50 States, 100 Days: The Book

By Chris Strub

To my Mom, Jane Strub.

I finally wrote it.

* * * * * * * * *

UPDATE, Feb. 2017: And printed it.

In Memory Of

Kim Wright Brown
Carolina Youth Development Center
8/17/1959 – 7/22/2016

Marilyn Doty Larson
Impression 5 Science Center
9/30/1942 – 5/13/2016

TABLE OF CONTENTS

Foreword
9

Madison WI 136	Peoria IL 140	Indianapolis IN 144
Lansing MI 148	Toledo OH 152	Pittsburgh 156
Binghamton NY 160	Burlington VT 164	Concord NH 168
Portland ME 172	Lowell MA 176	Providence RI 180
New Haven CT 184	Huntington NY* 188	Trenton NJ 193
Wilmington DE 197	Baltimore MD 202	Charlottesville VA 208
Charleston WV 212	Lexington KY 216	Asheville NC 220

FOREWORD

"Do, or do not. There is no try."

- Yoda

WATERTOWN, N.Y. – Chris Strub was born in Huntington Station, N.Y. on Aug. 23, 1985, to Jane and Charlie Strub.

Just kidding – let's save my life story for another day.

Instead, this book is about a 50-state, 100-day road trip – with a couple of flights mixed in.

The trip began May 15, 2015, from Greenville, S.C., and ended Aug. 21, in Asheville, N.C.

Along the way, I visited at least one different youth organization in each state.

This was my second trip around the United States. I also circled the continental U.S. during the summer of 2014, visiting 48 states in 90 days, without a tangible element of #SocialGood.

A few quick notes about the nuts and bolts of this book: each chapter begins with a photo from a visit, and the quote(s) that were written on my car in that city.

(Yes, written on my car – a 2007 Honda Accord whose continued health has been a godsend.)

The quotes are transcribed verbatim, exactly as they were written on the car, in removable paint marker. They are only attributed to the writer when the writer chose to sign his or her name. Most of, but not all, of the quotes were removed from the car on May 29, 2016.

This book was originally written as an eBook, so at the conclusion of each chapter, you'll see text teasing interviews done in that city: an "extended" interview, on YouTube; a Snapchat interview, on my Facebook page, as well as any media appearances I made during the stop. (Many of the media appearances are not linked because the news organizations chose not to publish the stories on their websites. Their loss, I suppose.)

Note that I am purposefully choosing to leave the text teasing these additional materials in the print copy of the book, with the hope that you'll look for some of the digital materials while reading.

The entire book was written in Watertown, N.Y., from Nov. 7 to Dec. 12, 2015, and it has not been subject to professional editing.

If an organization is of particular interest to you, I encourage you to watch the interview(s), and/or please consider volunteering and/or contributing. Every organization's website, listed by state, can be found on my website, www.TeamStrub.com.

You might be wondering why I went on this trip.

It's a question I ask myself every day, and I never come up with the same answer twice.

Maybe, as you read this book, you can help me figure it out. Send me a Tweet, or a SnapChat – @ChrisStrub – and I'll write back. Promise.

You might be wondering how I paid for this trip.

Painfully.

I spent the months leading up to the trip making pitch after pitch after pitch, leveraging contacts, following up and praying.

I thought I was close to a few different corporate sponsorships.

Instead, I truly believe the story to be stronger without one.

This book is about my story, at its core. No agendas, no politics, no pre-conceived notions, and no boss to report to.

This book is self-published because, after everything I went through to create this story, there wasn't a chance in hell I was going to let someone else's opinion decide whether it was worthy to sell.

This book is pure me. My heart, my soul, my all. One look at my credit card statements and I realize it's quite literally everything I've got.

And now, it's yours.

Enjoy.

Chris
@ChrisStrub

17

"EWOP"

- Kim

May 16, 2015 (State #1/50)

CHARLESTON, S.C. – "That's it?"

As Kim sat down at a picnic table about 30 feet from the stage, I saw her mouth those words, her face awash with disappointment.

I'd arrived at the Carolina Youth Development Center about 20 minutes prior. My phone was charged, my GoPro was ready, my bright yellow #TeamStrub t-shirt was pressed and clean – and inside, I was an utter basket case.

It was Day 2 of my grandiose attempt to change the world, one state at a time – and here I was, failing miserably, not a half-hour into my very first site visit.

I'd pulled my 2007 Honda Accord into the parking lot at the Carolina Youth Development Center with no idea of what to expect. The decal on the back window was still fresh -- 50 STATES OR BUST – but so far, all the ground I'd covered was in the Palmetto State.

So when Kim asked me to pull the car around so the kids could see, I happily obliged – even though there wasn't much of a spectacle.

The group was dancing and singing on the outdoor stage, and so I gathered all my courage and naivete and climbed right up there with them. Those small-group and one-on-one conversations would quickly become my favorite means of communication through the summer.

But on this day, the stage would be mine. Kim suggestively asked if I'd address the group. "Sure!" I said, as I immediately realized I had absolutely no idea what to say.

Kim cleared the stage of the children and enthusiastically introduced me, before stepping off stage to take a quick phone call.

"Hi everybody!" I said, or something disastrously milquetoast along those lines. "I'm Chris, and this summer I'm traveling around to all 50 states!"

The kids, ages seven to ten or so, looked at me like I had 12 heads.

One of the staff members took pity on me and raised her hand. "Why?"

I explained that I wanted to visit youths all around the country just like them, and that I was really excited to be starting here in my home state of South Carolina.

A couple of quick questions later – "are you going to Hawaii?" – and I was toast. The only thing standing between the kids and the nearby athletic courts was this pitiful excuse for a speech. I had nothing left and went, unauthorized, to the only line I could muster:

"Who wants to play some volleyball?"

Cue massive excitement from the kids – and the corresponding deflation from Kim.

"That's it?"

She mouthed it silently as I ashamedly slunk off the stage.

I felt, at that moment, every terrible emotion imaginable, the weight of 49 more inevitable failures crushing my hopes and dreams in the first hour of my very first visit.

Was I really bound to fail in all 50 states?

No. I wasn't going down that easy.

I joined the kids on the volleyball court for some fun in the sun.

I had a tremendously insightful conversation with Kim about the mission of the CYDC.

I helped the kids draw colorful maps of the United States, with questions for kids that I'd meet around the country at future visits.

I threw out the first pitch that night for the Charleston River Dogs, and successfully completed my first radio spot of the summer.

I earned back the respect of Kim, who went from "That's it?" to one of my best friends and biggest advocates.

And I turned a disastrous start to my day into a great success.

NEXT STOP: Savannah, Ga.

- - - - -

Kim Brown (10:35)

SnapChat Interview (0:59)

GREENVILLE NEWS: Greenville Man Embarks on Trip to 50 States in 100 Days to Help Nation's Youth

FOX CAROLINA: Upstate Man to Visit 50 States in 100 Days

GREENVILLE NEWS: Greenville Man Completes 50 -State, 100-Day Journey to Promote Volunteerism

2 - CHATHAM-SAVANNAH YOUTH FUTURES AUTHORITY

"Be respectful to everyone. Mrs. Broadie, Urban Hope Inc. Jack We love You"

May 18, 2015 (State #2/50)

SAVANNAH, GA. - She was so passionate, but so incredibly nervous.

Covardis Broadie is the site manager at Urban Hope Savannah, a ministry in downtown Savannah started 15 years ago by John "Jack" Roszkowiak.

In telling the story of Urban Hope, Mrs. Broadie – she prefers the courtesy title – could barely keep her emotions in check as she spoke of "Jack."

One thing I learned throughout my summer-long journey was that so many of the organizations I visited are the manifestation of one individual's passion and dreams.

But the one thing I learned in Savannah was how galvanized a staff can truly become after that founder passes away.

Jack died in January 2015 at the age of 83, but our conversation didn't center on Jack's death.

Instead, it centered on what Jack accomplished in his life, and specifically his 15 years of service to the organization now led by Mrs. Broadie.

With the cameras off, she shared with me numerous anecdotes about the youths that relied on Urban Hope throughout their adolescence and went on to succeed in college and beyond.

She spoke highly of the student leaders that worked their way through the program and now assist fellow youths.

She went out of her way to bring me back lunch from Subway as I worked on trying to clean up some of the kids' computers in the lab.

When we turned the camera on, her nerves emerged. In a way, I felt bad putting pressure on her to tell these stories to the world, with the news of Jack's passing still fresh on her mind.

But for all the pain the interview revisited, I also believe it was an important experience for both of us.

With Jack no longer around, his legacy truly lives on through the actions of Mrs. Broadie and her team. It would've been easy for Urban Hope to fold without Jack.

It would've been easy for Mrs. Broadie to give up on Urban Hope, without Jack to lead the way.

It would've been easy for me to not conduct an on-the-record interview with Mrs. Broadie.

And it would've been easy for me to write this column about my rather run-of-the-mill – though very informative -- meeting with the Chatham-Savannah Youth Futures Authority, another group I met with in Savannah earlier that day.

But we pressed on.

I believe encouraging Mrs. Broadie to speak about the new chapter for Urban Hope was healthy for her.

I believe telling the story of Urban Hope will inevitably help the youths in that program, who need those computers fixed; who need donations of food and other goods; who sorely need a bigger facility outside of the upper floor of the St. Paul CME Church.

I believe interviewing someone who was so nervous at the beginning of my trip allowed me the confidence to conduct interviews with all kinds of individuals the rest of the way.

And I believe, when Mrs. Broadie wrote "We love you Jack" in big script letters on the side of my car that morning, that his spirit, that had been so beneficial within the confines of those walls for 15 years, helped me succeed in visiting the remaining 48 states that awaited me in the months to come.

NEXT STOP: Jacksonville, Fla.

- - - - -

Covardis Broadie (9:18)

SnapChat Interview (2:11)

Curley Green & Tony Holmes (11:27)

SnapChat Interview (2:11)

3 - MALIVAI WASHINGTON YOUTH FOUNDATION

"Be the change. Volunteer – HandsOn Jacksonville"

"Call Your Mom!"

"Driving is more fun without a map! - Mark Kaye"

"Hope is the most important element of our endeavors. - Malivai Washington Youth Foundation, Jacksonville.*"

* Written by Chris (due to weather)

May 19, 2015 (State #3/50)

JACKSONVILLE, FL – Imminent danger on all sides.

It was a disturbing idea to internalize – that this beautiful facility I was touring was, as it was described to me, landlocked by perhaps the most dangerous neighborhood I'd visit all summer.

But for Executive Director Terri Florio, the daily risks quite literally came with the territory.

I'd been greatly looking forward to visiting the Malivai Washington Youth Foundation in Jacksonville – because I love tennis.

For the thousands of young people that have worked their way through MWYF over the years, they, too had developed a love of tennis – but under much different conditions than you and I.

High crime in zip code 32209 is no secret around Jacksonville. It's also the primary reason that founder Malivai Washington – he of early-90's professional tennis fame – chose West 6th Street to develop the foundation.

And so every day, attendees keep in the back of their mind the idea that at any given time, an emergency siren, immediately summoning everybody inside, could signal gunshots in the area.

To an outsider, it's a frightening, but distinguishing, wrinkle on a brilliant program.

So when I was offered a chance to go out and hit some balls with these bright, courageous kids – of course I accepted.

My shoes laced up, my antique racket twirling in my wrists, and a smile on my face, not once I did I think about the troubles that existed outside of the confines of the facility.

No, the only extenuating circumstances on this day were the brutal heat and overwhelming north Florida humidity.

We rallied for a while, played a few on-court games and excitedly watched the counselors exchange forehands before it was time to switch things up.

I was one of the last ones off the court, as the age groups traded places. Ironically, I was hesitant to leave the "fun" part of the activities – but the kids seemed to enjoy the in-classroom portion just as much.

After assisting with some homework help – an activity I'd become more accustomed to throughout the summer -- I even got a chance to read some Dr. Seuss to some of the younger children.

As evening approached, I was ready to call it an evening – but Mother Nature wasn't prepared to cooperate.

I stuck around for a bit longer and led the group in a high-spirited game of Simon Says, while one of the strongest thunderstorms I'd encounter all trip long blew through.

Thankfully, the downpour wasn't much of a harbinger; the vast majority of my trip would take place under brilliant sunshine.

The weather didn't diminish my bright memories of visiting the Mal Washington Youth Foundation. Through their Tennis & Tutoring program, they've positively changed the lives of thousands of young people who might otherwise fall into the trap of the troubles in the neighborhood.

Saying goodbye, as always, was tough, but I couldn't wait to continue my trip through the Southeast. Little did I know, two of my three favorite visits of the summer were on the horizon …

NEXT STOP: Montgomery, Ala.

- - - - -

Terri Florio & Sarah Kirkwood (10:05)

SnapChat Interview (1:37)

BONUS SnapChat Interview: Mark Kaye (1:17)

4 - EAT SOUTH

"Plant Hope. Fail Better. Dig Deeper."

May 21, 2015 (State #4/50)

MONTGOMERY, AL – You are what you eat – even on a 50-state, 100-day solo roadtrip.

Less than a week into my summer-long journey, my body was still in pretty good shape, but the predictable unpredictability of a drifter's diet was starting to set in.

A day with E.A.T. South was exactly what the doctor ordered.

Culinary considerations aside, my fourth stop had all the makings of a great day.

The state of Alabama is literally in my blood – my Dad was born in Selma, Ala., in January of 1952.

I had lined up my third first pitch of the summer – an evening date with the Montgomery Biscuits.

My visit even caught the attention of local officials: my day would start at Peter Crump Elementary School with an early-morning meet and greet with Mayor Todd Strange.

I rolled out of my hotel bed down to the continental breakfast – powdered donuts and orange juice, that I would've been smarter to skip. I even encountered my first cup of microwaveable grits, which I'd snag as more of a souvenir than for sustenance.

I made my way to Peter Crump to meet Liz Ellerson, a do-it-all AmeriCorps Vista whose passion for her cause was overshadowed only by her generous heart. (More on that in a minute.)

After the standard introductory pleasantries, we headed in to a small classroom being led by another Vista, Sarah Teel, who was leading a group in a discussion about fresh foods.

Luckily for me, the delicious-looking fresh foods on the table weren't all for naught. Squash, cherry tomatoes, plenty of kale — and, most appetizingly of all, farm-fresh eggs.

The Mayor and his assistant made an entrance just in time, as Sarah cracked the eggs on a heated George Foreman-type griddle. As he should, he politely greeted the children and the E.A.T. South reps first; I was very impressed when he knew Liz and Sarah by name. It was clear that Mayor Strange's knowledge and dedication to the program went much deeper than the occasional photo op.

When he turned to say hi to me, I was admittedly a bit starstruck. I was merely there to volunteer and help for a day — and here was the Mayor, expressing his sincere appreciation and even presenting me with a golden 'Montgomery' coin.

I snagged the Mayor for a quick SnapChat interview — surely his first experience with the medium — and even attempted to bait him into a hearty "Roll Tide" (which he expertly pivoted into a politically correct "Roll Eagle," splitting his on-camera endorsement between archrivals Alabama and Auburn.)

The classroom experience, topped off with a farm-to-table breakfast burrito, was just the beginning of what would be an epic day. We headed outside with Brandon, a newly hired E.A.T. South employee, to do some fingerpainting with cut-up vegetables from the garden, before Liz and I whisked off to visit the organization's storied downtown farm.

And if the in-classroom experience wasn't enough, the first impression at Montgomery's urban farm was just astonishing. Dozens of planters near the entrance are just the beginning of an enormous, public plot, managed by a gent named Jetson Brown. The crown jewel was, of course, the chicken coop — where Jetson let me gather some of those same eggs we'd prepared that morning.

The whole day was terrific — too much fun to fit into one column, in fact. Liz treated us to a food truck lunch – the Pimento BLT was top-5 foods I'd find all summer; we headed to E.A.T. South's other farm, several miles west of downtown, where I met and interviewed Catherine, and helped her plant some seeds, including sunflowers up front; later that evening, I'd be joined by Catherine, Jetson and Brandon at the Biscuits game, where I let Brandon throw out the first pitch in my place.

I had a spectacular time working with one of the best organizations in the country – and if that wasn't enough, the next day would bring me to another incredibly special city. And on I went …

NEXT STOP: New Orleans

- - - - -

Liz Ellerson & Jetson Brown (11:35)

SnapChat Interview (1:24)

BONUS SnapChat Interview - Mayor Todd Strange (1:14)

MONTGOMERY ADVERTISER: Traveling volunteer visits Crump Elementary

"From one New Yorker to another, I'm jealous of all your volunteer stops. Have fun and do great work. – Who Dat Jack #IAmVista

May 23, 2015 (State #5/50)

NEW ORLEANS – It wasn't the safest spot to park a car.

I followed Waze's directions to the dilapidated neighborhood in the heart of the Seventh Ward, and pulled up cautiously, about 100 yards down the road from the construction sites.

The heat and humidity that had drained so much of my energy in Jacksonville was back in a big way this morning, and I was donning, for the first time all summer, my bright yellow pants, ready to get to work.

I arrived almost simultaneously with the school bus full of youths – some of whom clearly had missed the "no open-toed shoes" part of the memo – and we gathered around to listen to Prince, the project leader for the day.

The mess that surrounded us was stark: on the near side of the road, two heavily damaged homes, tucked behind the nearly empty dumpster on the curb; across the street, a mostly empty lot, filled with rubble.

It was clear a terrible, terrible storm had wreaked havoc on this once-peaceful neighborhood; what isn't immediately apparent upon arrival, however, is the depressing notion that that storm occurred in 2005.

I've worked in the newspaper industry for most of my adult life, and so have written headlines about many a devastating hurricane.

But it's not until you step foot into the 7th Ward, now more than a decade after Hurricane Katrina blew through, that you fully understand how crushing a blast she was.

Surely, the young teenagers I would work alongside that day had little to no recollection of the chaos that tore through their home city in August '05.

But, through an opportunity offered by Youth Rebuilding New Orleans, this group – and scores of others throughout the years – would get a first-hand education in the effort needed to undo the extensive damage.

So after a brief explanation and safety briefing from Prince and the team, we were put to work.

Prince knew there would be an "individual volunteer" joining the kids that day, but unaware of my specific goals, offered me the opportunity to enter the damaged property and do some more advanced work with the staff.

I politely declined, instead choosing to get shoulder-to-shoulder with the kids, who were tasked with hauling debris from the nearly empty plot across the street to fill the dumpster.

We dove right in. Amusingly, the kids seemed to take the bayou humidity in stride much more easily than I; New Yorkers are used to a lot of things, but NOLA weather always gets me every time.

When YRNO's AmeriCorps Vista, Jack Styczynski, showed up on his bicycle about two hours later, we found a quiet spot to conduct an interview – behind another of the organization's projects, on the next block over.

I knew when I arrived in NOLA that it was a community that had a piece of my heart: I'd visited each of the previous two years, but both times for pleasure moreso than business.

This visit was completely captivating. Seeing, for the first time, the depth and complexity of the destruction from Katrina was mentality-changing. But as awful as it was, it was equally as energizing to see the optimism and motivation of the kids I was working alongside.

It was so inspiring, in fact, that when Jack and I wrapped up the interview before lunch – finishing the self-imposed "requirements" of my visit – I insisted on coming back after lunch to get some more work done in the house with Prince and the crew.

I loved YRNO, and that passion would stick with me all summer, to the extent that I'd repeatedly reference it as the most memorable experience I had on my trip.

With Memorial Day on the horizon, I'd spend a couple more days in NOLA, enjoying some quality time with good friends, getting a "5-minute Oil Change," sustaining a blown tire and visiting my first Hard Rock Cafe of the summer.

And when the sun rose on the holiday, I was rested, refreshed, and ready to roll North to my sixth state of the summer.

NEXT STOP: Jackson, Miss.

- - - - -

Jack Styczynski (13:46)
SnapChat Interview (1:40)

"Be active!"

"Your attitude determines your altitude."

"Don't be bound by fear!"

May 27, 2015 (State #6/50)

JACKSON, MS – "Up-Town, Funk You Up, Up-Town Funk You Up ..."

I was as energized as ever as I rolled up to the YMCA in Jackson, Miss.

People often asked how I picked the towns along my 50-state, 100-day journey, and quite honestly, I settled on Jackson thanks to the catchy refrain of Bruno Mars' smash hit "Uptown Funk."

"Harlem, Hollywood, Jackson, Mississippi ..." I sang along at the top of my lungs on the highway, as the ubiquitous tune played through my XM radio.

In all seriousness, it was tremendously invigorating to take a moment and think about how, at that moment, I was doing exactly what I wanted to be doing, exactly where I wanted to be.

The song concluded and it was time to get to work.

I headed inside to meet Kiersten Bullock – the quintessential southern belle if there ever was one. Incredibly kind and welcoming, Kiersten offered a quick tour of the relatively small facility before we threw on some plastic gloves and got to work.

The goal in my sixth state of the summer was to raise awareness for the summer feeding program, a statewide initiative that helps bring healthy food to hundreds of Mississippi's youth.

By all accounts, it was a tremendous success. Between preparing and packing messy sandwiches and portions of vegetables, I was sneaking glances at my email – and good news arrived just in time.

Two television stations expressed interest in covering my visit – to the delight of Kiersten, and the predictable chagrin of the shy kitchen staff.

They would be my first and second TV interviews of the summer, but far from the last. The evening anchors at WJTV had a bit of a field day with my last name – no shock there, either – but it was a joy to successfully raise awareness of the program, and let the community of Jackson know how they could help.

(You can watch my interview with WJTV on my Facebook page; the second interview seemingly never made it online.)

Logistics made it tricky for me to spend much time with the kids at the Y – we arrived during pool time, and I wasn't about to jump in; then I went inside with Kiersten to wrap up my interviews; then it started raining as I thought I might get to shoot some hoops – but it was a fun and productive day nonetheless.

With yet another minor-league baseball first pitch on my schedule that night, I headed back to the Cabot Lodge – a room graciously provided by the local CVB (thank you!) – took a deep breath and began researching the upcoming string of southern states that awaited.

NEXT STOP: Memphis

- - - - -

Kiersten Bullock (5:42)

SnapChat Interview (1:48)

WJTV: "One man's taking his mission to help nationwide"

"Big hearts build big dreams – be open."

"Life is a journey. Make everyday count. - @VolunteerMEM"

May 29, 2015 (State #7/50)

MEMPHIS – I honestly thought the dream was over.

Visiting a different youth organization in each state, over the course of 100 days, requires quite the broad skill set – dexterity, flexibility and, most importantly, attention to logistical detail.

While the idea for the trip probably came to me sometime around November 2014, the physical planning of the trip was in the works since February. Hundreds of emails, scores of phone calls and quite a bit of good luck were essential – and if you wanted to get in the door, you'd better have crossed your t's and dotted your i's.

Here I was in Memphis, in the parking lot at Big Brothers Big Sisters of the Mid-South, with undotted i's and uncrossed t's.

I knew this was the organization I wanted to visit. I knew the CEO, Adrienne Bailey, had expressed interest and agreed to host me for the morning.

But final confirmation – which, too often, came the night before a visit – never came.

I had no choice, of course, but to show up with my fingers crossed.

I sat silently in the parking lot, petrified that my 50-state volunteer quest would end unceremoniously in Tennessee. At least, I thought, I was relatively close to my vacant apartment in Greenville, S.C., and I could scuttle home with little trouble.

I picked up my iPhone one more time, opened my email and swiped down one more time; maybe the "see you soon!" I so desperately hoped for would magically appear.

Nothing.

But then. Reprieve.

"Chris?" came the thick southern accent, through my window.

It was Adrienne Bailey.

"Welcome to Big Brothers Big Sisters," she said.

And with that – a welcoming smile, a greeting and an invitation inside – all the stresses I'd been feeling just moments earlier disappeared.

As it turned out, the BBBS Memphis team was quite possibly the friendliest group I'd meet all summer. With their staff photos prominently posted on the wall, I learned that most of the senior staff here had been there for decades – an extremely stark contrast to the heavy turnover native to the nonprofit industry.

This would be the first of 10 chapters of Big Brothers Big Sisters I'd visit, and I entered with just about no knowledge of the organization. After helping unpack several large boxes of toys and trinkets, I subjected Susan to the most basic questions possible: what is Big Brothers Big Sisters?

How does the matching process work?

What sort of activities do matches engage in?

I soaked in as much knowledge as I could from this tremendous, award-winning chapter of what would become my favorite organization all summer. But nothing could prepare me for what happened next:

We wrapped up our interviews, gathered for a group picture, but before turning the camera on, Adrienne excused herself to grab something from her office.

An envelope. And a bag. She was smiling.

Adrienne silenced the room and presented me with a certificate … declaring me an "Honorary Big."

I'm not sure I could've smiled any broader. Hours earlier, I'd thought I wouldn't even be able to meet – turns out, they were even more prepared for my visit than I was. These were good, good people.

I was momentarily overwhelmed as she showed me the second part of the gift – a pair of Big Brothers Big Sisters dress socks.

We posed for a group photo, and I proudly held up the certificate that not only made my day, but made me a life-long fan of BBBS – and got me wondering how many more chapters I could visit before my trip ended.

NEXT STOP: Little Rock, Ark.

- - - - -

Adrienne Bailey & Susan George (9:24)

SnapChat Interview (1:06)

"Approach everyone with empathy and kindness."

May 30, 2015 (State #8/50)

LITTLE ROCK, Ark. – Fifty states in 100 days is a tricky thing to plan.

Visiting youth-related organizations around the country is an endlessly complicated endeavor – especially considering the construct of the modern week: five weekdays, buttressed by a two-day weekend.

Most nonprofits take a moment to breathe each week, especially on Sundays, and I certainly don't blame them. But the grueling nature of my 100-day gameplan had me searching for a youth-related nonprofit on a Sunday morning – the first Sunday visit of my trip.

As a homeless shelter, Our House in Little Rock is, by definition, operational 24/7, but none of its youth programming takes place on Sundays. So when I arrived at Our House to meet volunteer coordinator and AmeriCorps Vista Prentiss Jones, the facility was predictably quiet.

I was excited to meet Prentiss, who enthusiastically approved my visit well in advance. But when I arrived, I learned the young man was battling a nasty cold. Thankfully for me, he didn't cancel – as opposed to Memphis, where I worried my quest would unexpectedly end, a Sunday morning cancellation in Little Rock would've been disastrous for my nationwide plan.

What was terrific about this visit, though, was that the inactivity around the facility meant I could sit and truly learn from Prentiss what made the organization tick – and, on a deeper level, what homelessness is truly about.

It was clear, in spite of his sinuses, Prentiss was excited to dispel my misconceptions of the concept of homelessness. We chatted, off the record, for over an hour about how homelessness isn't as it's often portrayed in popular culture – instead, for the vast majority, it's a temporary condition onset by some combination of loss of employment and/or transportation.

This was my first experience with homelessness, but it wouldn't be my last – keep reading for tales from Portland, Tucson and Anchorage – and it was fascinating to let Prentiss destroy the naivete that saddled my mindset.

As interesting as our chat was, I hoped to see at least some of the expansive facility, including the child care area, so Prentiss led me around.

There were no kids around – they'd be back the next day, but I'd booked a travel day to Missouri – but we did encounter a couple of homeless adults milling around an enormous shared room, filled with beds.

When Prentiss keyed into a walk-in closet packed with dress clothes, we were joined by a remarkably gregarious gentleman with no shortage of stories to tell.

Boxed in by the confines of this small room, this man started telling Prentiss of his adventurous past marked by selling drugs, driving luxury vehicles and carousing with "the most beautiful woman you've ever seen."

The man seemed healthy, happy and with full control of his emotions, framing this story almost as if it was from a prior life, which actually made the whole thing more entertaining than sad.

I bore witness to this "conversation" for a few minutes, and it was quite the sight to see: a visibly ill Prentiss, tiredly nodding and acknowledging each wrinkle of this man's checkered past, the three of us uncomfortably crammed into the closet. (The idea crossed my mind to retrieve my phone to covertly live-stream this unusual situation, but I thought better of it.)

Eventually, Prentiss and I made our way outside to the Lindsey Robison Playground for a quick photo, and we wrapped up an abbreviated and kid-less, but enlightening and informational day. Prentiss was off to get some tea, Vitamin C and some well-deserved rest -- and I was on to Missouri.

NEXT STOP: Springfield, Mo.

- - - - -

<u>Prentis Jones (10:14)</u>

<u>SnapChat Interview (1:13)</u>

"Don't add sugar to your coffee."

June 1, 2015 (State #9/50)

SPRINGFIELD, Mo. – The reporter needed a few minutes to fully absorb the situation.

I welcomed Brett Martin to Big Brothers Big Sisters of the Ozarks, an organization his station had certainly covered before – but never in this scenario.

This was my second chapter of BBBS of the summer – having stopped in Memphis days earlier – and it felt great to have a first-hand understanding of the organization's structure before arrival.

And so when Brett Martin, a young, handsome reporter, rolled up, I was infinitely more comfortable in front of the cameras than I had been in Jackson, Miss., about a week earlier.

The folks from BBBS – Tyler Moles and Dylan McKinsey – were excited to see me, and had prepared a fun activity that I could help out with: donors had purchased commemorative engraved bricks to decorate the walkway to the building, and I'd been tasked to help the guys lay the bricks.

The goal of Big Brothers Big Sisters, of course, is to match adult mentors with children in need, for a period of at least a year – and in many cases, much longer. In many ways, my trip helped demonstrate the complex nature of volunteerism with each organization, because in addition to the long-term mentorship pairings, BBBS – and pretty much every other group I visited – can always use help with other responsibilities.

Brett -- who, unlike most of the TV reporters I'd encounter out west, arrived with an entourage of equipment and sound assistants – set up the shot outside the front of the building, seemingly in awe.

After a few minutes of bricklaying, I prepared for an interview – a process that ordinarily went hastily and without delay.

Brett, though, wasn't quite ready to turn the cameras on. The six of us stood around for a good fifteen minutes, chatting off the record about what had brought me to their small town – and the challenges that lay ahead.

Nine states in, I loved chatting about the trip – and it was clear that this TV reporter genuinely appreciated the story he'd stumbled upon that day. My goal all summer was to inspire people to get out and help in their own communities, and if Brett's well-produced spot on the news later that night wasn't enough, I had a feeling I'd inspired the reporter himself as well.

Looking back, commemorative brick-laying wasn't the most taxing activity all summer, but it was an honor to raise awareness not only for the organization, but for the dozens of generous donors whose ongoing support helps make their programming possible.

My only regret, per se, was not having the resources to invest in a brick of my own – but I promised myself that day that when I do someday make it to such a position, the kind and generous team at BBBS of the Ozarks would be right at the top of my list.

NEXT STOP: Wichita, Kan.

- - - - -

Tyler Moles & Dylan McKinsey (8:33)

SnapChat Interview (1:13)

OZARKSFIRST.COM: Traveling volunteer stops in Springfield

10 - AVID

"We have to make in ourselves what we expect in others. – @CMSPride"

June 2, 2015 (State #10/50)

WICHITA, Kan. – Math is a universal language – even out in rural Kansas.

I was very excited to make my first visit to Wichita and visit Coleman Middle School, the only school on my summer-long schedule.

In inquiring about what youth organization to visit in Kansas, all signs pointed to meeting Principal Jeff Freund and his highly acclaimed AVID program.

AVID, an acronym for Advancement Via Individual Determination, is a program woven into the fabric of intermediate schools around the United States.

As I'd learn on a blustery, sunny morning, the program primarily takes places during the academic year, but bridging the summertime learning gap was one major part of why Coleman's AVID program has garnered national recognition.

I ashamedly arrived at Coleman Middle School a little bit late, after a less-than-ideal night's sleep at an off-the-beaten-path motel the night before. (The only night all summer I'd wake up itchy – no fun.)

Thankfully, Mr. Freund and the welcoming crew he'd gathered – a math teacher and a model student – were cool with it, or at least pretended to be cool with it.

We spoke for a bit in the Principal's office before breaking out into my choice of classroom – naturally, I gravitated to math.

The kids were terrific. The class consisted of youths of different skill sets – some who'd been required to come to bring them up to speed, and some whose dexterity and thought processing clearly stood ahead. Only a handful of the youngsters were in the AVID program, but the entire group seemed to share the enthusiasm for learning.

Just a couple hours of classroom time for an old fogie like me was quite eye-opening. Although a lot of the methodology was familiar, what blew me away was the various types of hands-on tools the kids used to solve various problems.

One such contraption was a puzzle-type item, where the answers on a quiz corresponded to the sequence of blocks the kids had to arrange. Once all the responses were in place, the kids would flip the small plastic base over, revealing a design; if the image was symmetrical and sensible, the responses were confirmed; if not, the kids knew to keep working at it.

The instructors at CMS mixed in use of these tools with intensive, individualized help to keep the kids engaged with the subject matter without interruption for most of the class.

Without interruption, that is, except for the visitor bouncing around the room, SnapChatting, Instagramming and interviewing, trying to learn as much as he could about what made the program tick.

What brought the whole morning together was a game we played at the end of the session. We lined up in two groups of seven, across from one another, with our hands behind our backs. At the count of three, everyone would thrust their hands forward with a random number of fingers (1-10) extended. You and your opponent would compete to see who could complete the multiplication problem faster – and the winner would keep his spot in line, while the loser moved to the end.

As would be the case in most other states, the kids mostly beat me at their own game, taking well-deserved pride in beating the fun-loving guest.

It was a joy spending a few hours with "D" and all the kids at CMS; my only regret is that I arrived on the same day a Sam's Club and a new terminal at the Wichita Airport were opening, which meant no mainstream media.

No matter. TV cameras or not, the time I spent at Coleman was equally memorable for me as I hope it was for the kids. And looking ahead, I still had 40 states left to tackle.

NEXT STOP: Oklahoma City

- - - - -

Jeff Freund (11:53)

SnapChat Interview (1:53)

WICHITA PUBLIC SCHOOLS: Coleman's Math Academy Has a Special Visitor

11 - SUNBEAM FAMILY SERVICES

"Trust your crazy ideas!"

June 4, 2015 (State #11/50)

OKLAHOMA CITY – Too often this summer, during my site visits, I found myself in the spotlight.

At Sunbeam Family Services in Oklahoma City, I was more than delighted to give it up.

More on that in a moment.

I was greeted at Sunbeam by Erin Engelke, a super-sweet Southern Mom with an enormous heart.

It was always nice working with organizations large enough to have someone like Erin, whose role allowed her the opportunity to spend some time giving an informational tour and letting me truly experience all the different aspects of the organization.

In reality, it probably would've taken me closer to a week to gain a full appreciation of everything taking place at Sunbeam, which offers a huge variety of services, as CEO Jim Priest would explain, "from cradle to cane."

With the focus of my summer-long quest on youth services, Erin designed a day that would allow us to focus on their Educare program, while also hearing about everything else going on there.

She took me on a quick tour of the neighborhood, past the building that Sunbeam had called home for many decades, as we headed to the Educare facility.

I was very impressed by the playground facilities behind the building – doubling back to snag a selfie before we headed back inside – but the true fun of this day came when Erin brought me in to work with some of the kids in the program.

The first room we visited was a younger group, who were working hard on simple arts and crafts. I took a seat amongst the kids on a chair about 8 inches off the group and about 6 inches wide – not truly designed for a 6', 175-pound millennial – and got to work on building my own popsicle-stick airplane.

With the glue drying, I chose to color the sticks bright orange and baby blue – the signature colors of the heart and soul of the town, the Oklahoma City Thunder. (Erin spoke very highly of "Russell," Westbrook, of course, a major supporter of Sunbeam.)

I didn't collect a lot of souvenirs this summer, but as I write this, my popsicle-stick airplane sits on my mantle, a reminder of a morning that would become even more memorable for the next room we'd visit.

Erin asked me if I'd be comfortable reading to the next group – slightly older – and, of course, I obliged.

I took a seat on the (slightly larger) chair at the front of the class, and the kids (and staff members) respectfully quieted down to listen as I read.

When we reached the end of the book, and made it through the perfunctory polite applause, a couple of the kids asked if we could read another. I glanced at Erin to check on the time constraints – she nodded approvingly – and an adorable little girl asked if she could choose the second book.

Not wanting to make the other kids jealous, I paused, but when none balked, I acquiesced. She stood up, walked past me to the stack of books behind me, picked one out and pivoted back to the front of the group.

I extended my hand, cleared my throat and prepared to reprise my role as the reader … but this young woman had a different idea.

She swung open the cover of the book, as only a five-year-old can, and started reading, as I sat in front of the group, swallowing an enormous grin.

Predictably, she couldn't quite captivate the audience as I had, but Erin and the staff couldn't contain their laughter as I patiently watched this go-getter take the stage.

When she was done, Erin and I scuttled back to the main office for lunch – gourmet take-out pizza in a conference room, with the CEO, the outgoing chair of the Board of Directors, and leaders from each department of the multi-faceted organization.

It was an honor to spend some time with the senior leadership of Sunbeam – and just as enjoyable to see one of our future leaders take charge during a summertime reading session.

NEXT STOP: Austin, Texas

- - - - -

Jim Priest & Erin Engelke (11:02)
SnapChat Interview (1:43)

12 - BOYS & GIRLS CLUB

"Make the most of each day, as it is a gift from above."

June 4, 2015 (State #12/50)

AUSTIN, Texas – It was the first real moment that I could sit back and say, "This is already a huge success."

Part of my preparation to visit each state was to reach out to local media. My overarching goal all summer was to shine a bright light on the best organization in each city I visited, and leave each time having raised awareness in the community of the cause at hand.

Austin was one of the main reasons I wanted to go on a second trip in the first place. After my 2014 tour of 48 states in 90 days, the one city I really regretted missing out on was Austin. (I'd visited Houston and Dallas.)

Before visiting the Boys & Girls Club of Austin, I actually spent a couple of days holed up in San Antonio, where the hotel rates were slightly cheaper, and I had a free meal awaiting at the Hard Rock Cafe.

I made my way back north to Austin to meet Club Director Steve Zuniga. As it turned out, my visit coincided with the first day of summer programming at this location.

That sounds crazier than it actually was, because the chapter I'd been directed to is a relatively small arm of the much larger BGC Austin family. Meadowbrook Apartments is a 160-unit complex in east Austin, run by the city's housing authority.

Many of the facilities I'd encounter this summer had advanced technology ensuring a strong perimeter, ostensibly keeping the children safe; my visit today was, oddly, quite the opposite.

Because all the children in the program were residents of the apartment complex, they were more or less free to come and go. Steve mentioned that once a child left the club for the day, he or she wasn't permitted back until the following day, but that rule seemed loosely enforceable.

Texas was my eleventh state of the summer, but this was my first Boys & Girls Club – perhaps the most omnipresent youth organization in the country.

Steve turned out to be the perfect ambassador, and it was very interesting to see a particularly multicultural group in action. While it seemed a handful of the kids spoke at least some Spanish, there were two young girls who separated themselves from the English speakers.

With several years of junior high school Spanish hidden somewhere in my brain (Holá, Senor Gavilan!) I did my best to comfort and converse with the understandably shy pair.

Luckily, Steve's bilingual skills far outpaced mine, and as he laid out the ground rules and parameters for the summertime program, he was careful to intertwine a bit of Spanish. When he wrapped up his pitch, he walked over to the two young girls, crouched down and made sure they were comfortable with everything he'd said.

I knew from that moment Steve's heart was genuinely in the right place, which made it immensely satisfying a couple hours later, when the local news showed up to speak with me. After they wrapped my interview, I strongly suggested they take a moment to interview Steve, whose eyes lit up at the suggestion.

As the one-man news "crew" brought Steve outside and hooked the microphone to his collar, I slipped out behind him, to watch quietly while the bright lights shined in his visage.

And as fun as it was to be interviewed and explain my story from state to state, some of the best feelings of the summer came from seeing that spotlight shined away from me and onto the folks who really make a long-standing difference for all the kids – just like Steve.

It was mission: accomplished – and it was a feeling I'd experience again, in the days and weeks to come.

NEXT STOP: Las Cruces, NM

- - - - -

Steve Zuniga (8:01)

SnapChat Interview (1:40)

BONUS SnapChat Interview: Save the Children (0:49)

13 - BBBS MOUNTAIN REGION

"Unless someone like you cares a whole awful lot, nothing is going to get better. It's not. – Dr. Seuss"

June 7, 2015 (State #13/50)

LAS CRUCES, NM – It was unquestionably the lowest point of the summer.

I don't know what came over me that night, but I emotionally melted down.

It happens to the best of us, and quite frankly, in retrospect, I'm astonished it didn't happen to me more often.

But the night before my visit to Big Brothers Big Sisters of the Mountain Region was the weakest I'd ever felt.

I was a wreck, a total mess, and the last thing I needed was to be anywhere near a camera.

It was a long, a very, very long, drive from Austin to Las Cruces, and the stark reality of having to do all of this on my own was starting to set in.

Fuel was expensive. Food wasn't cheap. Hotels were adding up – this was still weeks before I conceded that I could sleep in my car.

I'd been incredibly fortunate that several cities across the Southeast were gracious enough to offer lodging assistance – but I was quickly learning that that would not be the case across the rest of the country. And with three-quarters of my trip remaining, I already sorely missed the southern hospitality.

I pulled my car into the parking lot of a hotel I was not booked at, took a deep breath – and started crying.

In a summer that was filled with color, I posted an emotional black-and-white photo on my Instagram account, the starkest image of how one man, 50 states, 100 days wasn't always so rosy. I even insinuated that I might give up on the trip after Las Vegas.

And then I pulled myself together.

I wasn't a quitter.

I wasn't about to make it 25% of the way through a life-long dream and give up.

And, more than anything, I wasn't going to let my emotions get the best of me the next morning with Dawn at BBBS.

It turned out to be a great visit. We met at La Posta de Mesilla, a famous Mexican spot in the heart of Las Cruces, where Dawn was the "keynote" speaker at a local Rotary Club meeting. We got to sit up at the front of the room, and I still think it was probably the only Meerkat live-stream in the history of Rotary Club. (I have to wonder what viewers worldwide thought of the singing ...)

It was a very busy day for the very small BBBS team, so it was very kind of Dawn to set aside some time to conduct interviews and hang out with me for a bit. Later that evening, BBBS had a booth set up at a street fair just down the road from the office – another fun opportunity to live-stream from a corner of the world most will never get to experience.

With my spirit still a little shaken after my mental breakdown the night before, that street fair quickly restored my confidence. Broadcasting from my iPhone, I interviewed Dawn and her board chairman, Lucas, taking questions from a worldwide audience and conveying them to a pair of passionate nonprofit ambassadors.

In Southern California, my friend George – whom I knew only through this digital platform – was watching intently, and when I prompted the audience for questions for Dawn and Lucas, he seemed more interested than most in the ins and outs of the organization.

I quickly sweetened the pot, challenging George that if the stream picked up a handful of "re-streams" – nerd speak for people sharing the link on their own channels – he take the initiative to sign up to be a big. To my delight, he did – and at my urging, the audience followed suit.

When George commented that he'd gone on the site to fill out the form, my confidence rebounded from an all-time low the night before to an all-time high. Together, the technology and my spirit had created tangible change.

We retreated to the office, where Dawn inscribed a Dr. Seuss quote on a backseat window and bid me farewell.

I turned the ignition, returned to the highway and headed westward into the sunset – with no semblance of a finish line in sight.

NEXT STOP: Tucson, Ariz.

- - - - -

Dawn Starostka (12:26)

SnapChat Interview (1:25)

LCSUN-NEWS.COM: Big Brothers Big Sisters Hosts Traveling Volunteer

"When life gets tough … keep going!"

June 9, 2015 (State #14/50)

TUCSON – The proverbial heat was on as my westward trek brought me to Arizona.

Little did I know I was about to step into one of the fastest-growing youth organizations in the United States.

Youth On Their Own was my second homelessness organization of the summer, after a brief Sunday stop at Our House in Little Rock several weeks prior.

Staff turnover is relatively common amongst all nonprofits. What's not common is exponential staff growth, especially in a medium-sized city like Tuscon.

But I'd quickly learn, in a terrific interview with Program Director David Martin, that YOTO was pushing all the right buttons – and that the key to their success wasn't even really a secret.

That key?

Simplicity.

YOTO's mission is to support the high school graduation of homeless youth in Tucson.

And, as Dave would explain to me, the reason they're so good at achieving that goal – is, quite simply, because they keep the focus on that one goal.

Youth On Their Own is – for the moment – located in a relatively small building, but it is almost comically packed with employees.

When the staff was summoned to take a group picture outside with me – a fairly common occurrence as the summer went on – I couldn't believe how many people were heading down the stairs.

With my complex trip beginning May 15, I had begun outreach, especially to the earlier cities, as early as late February. Amusingly, Volunteer Administrator Emerson Kuhn would explain to me, my visit request had not only pre-dated his hiring – but also the hiring of Martin, the voice of the organization and the gentleman I'd interview.

When I was introduced to Kristyn Conner, one of the organization's grant writers, I shouldn't have been surprised to see her sharing an office with another writer (who wasn't there); by the time you read this, I wouldn't be surprised to hear a third or even fourth person might be sharing their space as well.

All this organizational growth was obviously indicative of success, which Martin was quick to back up with plenty of supportive data.

And although I didn't get to work with youths on this day, I was invited to perform some volunteer tasks in YOTO's famed "Mini Mall."

When you hear "Mini Mall," it's probably nothing like you imagine it in your head. The "mall" is about 12 shelves full of foodstuffs, toiletries and some clothing, with a big scale strategically in the middle.

Tucson's homeless youths are invited to come collect 10 pounds or less of items per week, under the supervision of staff. Volunteers – like myself – help keep the shelves stocked by refilling items from a room full of inventory, mere steps away from the "mall" portion.

It was simple yet effective – a terrific change of pace, and a really tremendous model that, as Martin was sure to mention, would be a great addition to almost every community in the country.

I'd return to the theme of homelessness in a couple weeks in Portland – but for now, it was time to soldier on to the biggest city on the entire itinerary.

NEXT STOP: Los Angeles

- - - - -

David Martin (13:53)
SnapChat Interview (1:40)

15 - A PLACE CALLED HOME

"Inspiration exists, but it has to find you working."

"Give without expecting anything in return. – @Sacca"

"Don't let your zip code determine your destiny."

"This trip will soon be history. Make it famous history! - Your cousin Aleks"

June 12, 2015 (State #15/50)

LOS ANGELES – One might think that in a city of 3.8 million people, it'd be simple to find a youth nonprofit seeking volunteers.

Not the case.

A Place Called Home, in South Central L.A., ended up getting the nod after many weeks of endless searching.

Throughout my trip, I mostly kept to mid-size or smaller cities, passing up Chicago for Peoria; Boston for Lowell; Dallas for Austin; and so on. But in sketching my schedule, and after a southwestern string where I passed up on Phoenix and Albuquerque for Tucson and Las Cruces, I was ready for the bigtime.

Little did I know, when I walked into A Place Called Home, that this relatively small kitty-cornered facility was responsible for so much wonderment all summer long.

For those unfamiliar, South Central Los Angeles is not the most affluent part of town, and it was eye-opening to learn that APCH provides their programming at no cost to families.

What really blew me away was when Ana Maria Perez Paulino mentioned that children in the program would be taking nearly 100 field trips that summer.

Luckily for me, there were some kids on the campus to hang out with, and after the standard introductory pleasantries, Ana Maria brought me over to art class, with Art Director Bernyce Talley.

The kids were preparing to put on a Star Wars-themed production, and our big goal on this day would be to paint the R2D2 they'd recently pieced together.

This was no small task – the contraption was almost as tall as I was!

Luckily, there was no shortage of paint.

Donning a smock for the second time during the summer – the first was, of course, in Alabama – I didn't do as much painting as I did stand above and steady the canvas for the enthusiastic kids below.

It never made the experience any less fun, but it was a bit more awkward to try and capture a visual while visiting organizations that didn't allow the kids to be photographed. I snuck a quick selfie here and there, but the hectic nature of our painting project meant pictures were hard to come by.

And although my volunteer experience was limited to the painting project, it was clear just by chatting with Ana Maria that the scope of APCH is immense. Since launching in 1993, the staff has grown to dozens, with titles like "Master Gardener," "Dance Coordinator" and "Digital Media Instructor" that demonstrate their immense diversity of programming.

My time in Southern California wasn't limited to just APCH; I was able to visit family in San Diego, meet up with some live-streaming friends in Santa Monica, and visit a pair of SoCal's three Hard Rock Cafe locations. But after one final stop, at In 'N' Out Burger, I was thrilled to be heading East for the first time in a while.

NEXT STOP: Las Vegas

- - - - -

Ana Maria Perez Paulino (8:39)

SnapChat Interview (1:09)

16 - OPPORTUNITY VILLAGE

Photo Courtesy Mignon Lazatin / Opportunity Village

"Failure is the only opportunity to begin again – just more wisely."

June 14, 2015 (State #16/50)

LAS VEGAS – Not all nonprofits are created equal.

As I re-live my summer, state by state, some memories are more fond to recall than others.

And while I try to recap each visit in a similar number of words, I feel like I could write all night about my time at Opportunity Village in Las Vegas.

No organization made me feel quite as welcome as OV. For months in advance, their social media/communications department was keeping in touch, going through the trouble of creating and distributing their own customized press release (which even got picked up by Robin Leach!).

And for everything I read about OV before my visit, it was all of that and more. As I look back at my entire summer, my other two favorite organizations – E.A.T. South in Montgomery, Ala., and Youth Rebuilding New Orleans – were right at the beginning of my trip, leaving me not fully prepared to take in and appreciate the experience.

By the time I pulled up to OV, I was confident, ready, and well-prepared.

… That is, until I arrived.

Special Events Manager Veronica Atkins – an absolute angel if there ever was one – had planned a full day of fun activities for me, starting right off the bat with a sit-down interview with venerable CEO Ed Guthrie.

I was so excited to meet this man, and hear of his decades of experience at the helm – that I mis-read Veronica's final email to me, and promptly showed up at the wrong campus.

Immediately, all of the enthusiasm and energy I'd built up went out the window.

Embarrassed to no end – I was keeping the CEO himself waiting!! – I sprinted back to my car, frantically emailing Veronica a slew of apologies while trying to remember that, hopefully, everything would be okay.

Channeling my inner New Yorker as I drove, er, assertively to the correct location, nothing, I decided, could ever come easy to me. Just when you think you're in a position to succeed, the rug can come right out from underneath you.

But from the moment I walked in and met Veronica, I knew everything was going to be fine.

Flustered, I still managed to bungle my interview with Ed, who graciously agreed to still take the meeting despite me being nearly 30 minutes late. Lacking composure for what surely would've been one of the best interviews of the summer – he was great – is still, to this day, one of my biggest regrets.

But neither Veronica nor I would allow my tardiness to detract from what would truly become a life-changing day.

I met Jesse, the leader of the famed "OV Elvi," an all-Elvis tribute dance troupe that is one of many incredibly memorable wrinkles in the fabric of OV.

I met Darryl Borges, the organization's music director, who performs regularly himself under the bright lights of Vegas, but eloquently explained that his time sharing his gifts with the OVIP's is immensely more satisfying.

I met Steve Koontz, OV's smooth-talking Director of Event Operations, and learned a lot about the one-of-a-kind Magical

Forest.

But most importantly, I met dozens of wonderful individuals with intellectual disabilities who were delighted to let me bring some well-deserved attention to the terrific work they do every single day.

I spent two days in Las Vegas and neither placed a single bet, nor had a single drink on the strip – and it was unquestionably the highlight of my 50-state journey. Before I even pulled away from OV, I knew it was a spot that I wanted to visit again sometime.

NEXT STOP: Salt Lake City

- - - - -

Ed Guthrie (14:05)

SnapChat Interview (1:59)

FOX 5 LAS VEGAS: Chris Strub Visits the Magical Forest

"Help others grow"

"Don't be afraid to dream. Follow your inspirations. - Dylan"

June 18, 2015 (State #17/50)

SALT LAKE CITY – I went from the largest organization I discovered all summer in Las Vegas, to the smallest one all summer, in Salt Lake City.

U.T.A.H. Gardens is the brainchild of former SLC city councilman Shane Siwik, whose penchant for urban gardening is rivaled only by his determination to stay out of the way of his group's youth leadership.

Siwik had insisted on picking me up from my hotel and driving me to the urban farm, in nearby Magna – an unusual request, considering my car was a bit of a spectacle by this point.

When we reached the plot, Siwik introduced me to the group and then almost immediately bowed out of the discussion, handing the reins to Connor, a youth who claimed to be in charge of the gardens.

Connor was admittedly a bit shy, but in speaking to him one-on-one, you could tell he had a solid understanding of what was needed to raise a successful crop.

He led us through an old gate and around a corner to a plot about 1/5 the size of what I'd seen at E.A.T. South in Montgomery, Ala. About six large beds in a row sat adjacent to a large, open field, that held one lonely horse.

There was work to be done, for sure, but it seemed to me that it was more important to Siwik that Connor take the lead on the project than it was for the work itself to get done.

And so, at Siwik's urging, Connor re-convened the group to explain what needed to be done, before heading back – at Siwik's request – to bring over the tools necessary for us to do the work.

It was all very curious to watch. You could tell Siwik knew exactly what needed to be done that day, and in observing the plot as a whole, you could also tell that perhaps this wasn't the first time the group's leader had taken a laissez faire approach.

But even from the time we rolled up to the moment we wrapped up, you could clearly see an improvement in Connor's confidence. Siwik's insistence that Connor be the one to lead showed that, without a doubt, he prioritized empowering the youths over the success of the garden itself.

That's not to say Siwik's presence wasn't felt. About midway through the morning, he asked the group to come together so he could explain some of the science behind the work we were all doing that day. He parlayed the technical discussion into a bit of a sales pitch, reminding all the youths in attendance – some veterans, and some first-timers – how they could help the group grow by recruiting friends to join them for their next session.

And before the group broke for the day, Siwik could be seen having a productive discussion with Simran, Jessica and Connor, the group's senior student leadership, about their plans for growth for the upcoming school year.

I tried, this summer, to remember one big take-away from each visit I made. In Salt Lake City, more than any other stop all summer, Siwik's determination to empower the youths in the group made a lasting impression.

NEXT STOP: Boise, Idaho

- - - - -

Shane Siwik (12:21)

SnapChat Interview (1:45)

18 - GIRLS ON THE RUN

"Keep on running!"

June 21, 2015 (State #18/50)

BOISE, Idaho – In visiting 50 states in 100 days, I came across a handful of truly national organizations.

The YMCA, The Boys & Girls Club of America and, of course, Big Brothers Big Sisters, all can be found in all 50 U.S. States.

In my 18th state of the summer, I came across another "national" organization, one that was certainly close to my heart – Girls On The Run.

It was a beautiful, sunny Fathers' Day in western Idaho, and GOTR of the Treasure Valley Executive Director Melissa Bixby had very kindly agreed to take some time away from her family that morning to tell me all about her great organization.

We convened at a playground in her neighborhood to sort some flash cards for an activity her group would be working on later in the season.

I streamed our discussion about the organization live on Meerkat, allowing a global audience to join us at a quiet Idaho picnic table.

And as we talked through the ins and outs of the brand, Melissa mentioned that in addition to Idaho, Girls on the Run was active in 48 other states.

Wait – 48?

Indeed – I had encountered a national organization with just one chink in its armor. Girls on The Run proudly features chapters in 49 out of 50 U.S. states.

For a young man weaving his way through all 50, this idea blew my mind. How could a national organization allow for one state to hold out? Especially an organization whose principles – teaching elementary-age girls crucial life skills through running – resonated so universally?

Endlessly curious, I did some quick research and found out that the lone holdout state still lay ahead for me this summer …

Wyoming.

How in the world could Wyoming, of all places, not have a chapter? In my travels during the summer of 2014, I developed a strong affinity for the Cowboy State, having made stops in great cities like Rawlins, Rock Springs and Green River.

Later this summer, I'd scheduled a day in the state capitol – Cheyenne – and knew I'd have to re-visit the idea of bringing this important organization to the Equality State.

But enough about Wyoming! I had a terrific time learning all about Girls on the Run with Melissa. And although I'd pledged before the summer started that I wouldn't spend more than one day with each group – a groundrule in place to help me maintain energy levels and sanity – when Melissa offered to convene the group the next morning for a run, I couldn't say no.

Although unable to stay in Boise – my weekend visit coincided with a massive youth soccer tournament that sapped every hotel in the metro area – I found a cozy room in nearby Caldwell, and set my alarm real early to get back and run with Melissa and the crew.

The run, along and across the Boise River, was cathartic and energizing, and it was great fun to meet, and jog alongside, a handful of enthusiastic youths and local GORT board members.

It was also a perfect farewell to the third-largest city in the Northwest, as I climbed back behind the wheel for one of my longest drives yet – off to beautiful Portland.

NEXT STOP: Portland, Ore.

- - - - -

Melissa Bixby (12:55)

SnapChat Interview (1:38)

"When you need help, there's a community waiting for you. Go find them! ~ New Avenues Loves You"

June 24, 2015 (State #19/50)

PORTLAND – My body was in Oregon, but my mind couldn't help but focus on Alaska.

I'd just completed the lengthy drive all – and I emphasize ALL – the way across the beautiful state of Oregon, from Boise to Portland.

I love Portland; in fact, I'd confidently call it my second-favorite U.S. city. I very nearly moved to Portland in 2014, before deciding upon Greenville, S.C.

But this summer, I was scheduled to visit all 50 U.S. states – the 48 that I was familiar with, plus Hawaii and Alaska.

And as I pulled into downtown Portland, under predictably cloudy skies, my mind was fixated on my upcoming flight to Anchorage.

Nevertheless, I was excited to visit New Avenues for Youth, a leading shelter in a city nationally recognized for its homelessness programs.

I was greeted by Sama Shagaga, a bright-eyed young man eager to show off the facility.

One of the distinguishing marks about NAFY was its multifaceted setup, which both encouraged visitors to take advantage of all the programming offered there, while discouraging crowds from idly sitting by.

Sama proudly took me through an impressive classroom setup, buttressed by a state-of-the-art computer lab.

I'm never one not to ask questions, and I took on a big one right off the bat: if all of these valuable, tangible resources are dedicated to individuals who have seemingly lost everything in their lives, isn't there a constant urge to steal?

Sama offered a modestly conciliatory nod, and explained the natural camaraderie that the homeless youth shared – just as they shared the facility itself.

NAFY was my second homeless shelter of the summer, and it was clear I still had much to learn.

Sama led us back upstairs, where we concluded the brief tour at the entrance to the career education department, where he explained that he spent most of his days.

As important as it was for New Avenues to provide food and shelter to the homeless, it seemed equally important to offer job counseling.

Director of Development Jessica Elkan would explain, during a broad-ranging and informative interview (which, of course, you can view on my YouTube channel) that professional training and job placement were crucial parts of ensuring that the youths in NAFY's care were put back on a path to success.

But as much as I learned from Sama and Jessica – who, in moments of levity, also informed me that Portland is nothing like the popular series Portlandia – it was eye-opening to spend some time downstairs as staffers served breakfast to the youths.

Tracked loosely by a paper sign-in sheet, every youth who entered was known by name, and many of them seemed familiar with one another.

I came prepared to help prepare breakfast, and NAFY has a full, professional kitchen setup at the ready, but my visit coincided with cereal day, which minimized the labor aspect.

I did get to say good morning to a few of the youths, most of whom were either in engaged conversation with a friend, or sat alone, looking like they preferred isolation.

I might've stuck around longer, but with my mind caught up in Anchorage, I wrapped the interviews, called it a day and continued on to the North.

NEXT STOP: Anchorage

- - - - -

Jessica Elkan (13:24)

SnapChat Interview (1:46)

20: COVENANT HOUSE

"I maintain the power to define who I am.*"

"Do not let anyone define you, who you will become, the kind of parent you will become. Only you have that right.*"

*Written by Chris (geography)

June 23, 2015 (State #20/50)

ANCHORAGE – I wasn't expecting this conversation to be the most memorable part of my first visit to Alaska.

I had just wrapped up a terrific extended chat with Carlette Mack, COO of Covenant House Anchorage – one of the fastest-growing organizations I'd come across all summer.

And I was on my way to the Passage House – a home for single mothers in need of respite and time to get their lives on track.

I was tasked with pulling weeds and spreading mulch outside of the home – a decidedly American assignment in a state that felt a lot more "normal" than I'd anticipated.

But before I left the main facility at Covenant House, I asked the brilliant COO if anyone else there would like to chime in for my SnapChat interview.

She paused, just for a moment, and led me back to the desk to the young, dark-haired woman who'd welcomed me about an hour earlier.

Her name was Jenny, and as Carlette made the re-introduction – of course, I'd offered pleasantries when I first arrived – you could instantly tell that Jenny was eager to tell her story.

With my signature America East backpack slung over my shoulders, I joined Jenny in a small room nearby and quickly called up SnapChat.

Having landed a great interview with Carlette, I only needed a couple of quick clips from Jenny, so she could get back to work and I could make it on time to the Passage House.

But when I explained to Jenny my project, and what had brought me to Anchorage, her eyes lit up.

As with the vast majority of my interactions this summer, this was a private, one-on-one chat, far from the glitz and glamor of the television cameras.

She recognized my mission was to help her tell her story, even if we had to squeeze it into 10-second bursts.

I have no doubt I could've sat there all day with Jenny, to explore the true depth of these seven words:

"I was a kid at Covenant House."

The most powerful stories I came across all summer always seemed to come from those who had personally worked their way through the program, and Jenny was a prime example.

"Covenant House gave me a chance to succeed, and now I want to give back to the youth that are here now."

One five-minute conversation – and one 10-second clip, which remains saved on my (very full) iPhone – made a lasting impression on me, even more than the immense beauty of downtown Anchorage; even more than my first taste of fresh-caught Alaskan salmon; even more than the insanity-inducing sunlight that kept me awake beyond midnight.

And so as I slept in the back seat of my rented car that "night" – the first time I'd ever slept in a car, and it wasn't even my own, and can you even call it "night" in Alaska? – I was immensely thankful.

I was thankful for every material possession I had; thankful that my credit card limit allowed me to even rent a $200-a-day car; and thankful that I'd met Jenny Lachance, whose determination to help others who are struggling as she had proved to me that there is hope for our next generation.

NEXT STOP: Honolulu

- - - - -

<u>Carlette Mack (11:55)</u>

<u>SnapChat Interview (1:52)</u>

.

21: BBBS HAWAII

"Focus on enhancing the good, instead of righting the wrongs.*"

"Live PONO!*"

* Written by Chris (geography)

June 30, 2015 (State #21/50)

HONOLULU – The best moments of my first-ever visit to Hawaii came not on a beach, at a club, or even at my hostel – but in closed meeting rooms with two extraordinary people.

First, Kaulana.

Of course, I'd been preparing to get to Hawaii for as long as I'd been planning my trip.

I'd done extensive outreach with the Hawaii CVB, filling out lengthy forms to request travel assistance. I knew visiting Hawaii without any financial sponsorship would be crushing.

So when the reply came back, "sorry, there's nothing we can do for you," my spirit was only galvanized.

As long as I could find the perfect youth organization to work with in Honolulu, I knew everything I invested in this journey would be well worth it.

And the moment I sat down with Kaulana Chang, that feeling came to fruition.

The summer of 2015 was a game-changer for the LGBT community in the United States. On June 25 – just days before my flight to Honolulu – the U.S. Supreme Court had struck down a ban on gay marriage.

(By the way, I sincerely hope someone reads this in 50 years and laughs that a gay marriage ban was still a thing way back then.)

It was also a rough time for GSA Hawaii, Kaulana's one-man-show that helped inspire and grow GSA's around the state. The funding for GSA Hawaii had been cut, as of July 1 – the day after we were to meet.

I couldn't get in touch with Kaulana, try as I might, and so I made a Hail-Mary visit to his office – where he was nowhere to be found. Huge bummer.

I started walking back towards my hotel, and summoned my phone to send a disappointed SnapChat or two explaining the situation.

And then my phone rang.

Kaulana.

On the final afternoon before his organization completely ran out of funding, Kaulana was willing to spend some time with me, to allow me to tell the world about the GSA.

And tell the world we did!

With an interesting multi-piece rig featuring my iPhone, my iPad and my GoPro staked to my selfie stick, we set up a makeshift broadcasting studio and staged an hour-long "telethon," giving Kaulana a platform to tell his story and make a direct plea to the entire world to help show their support. Any contributions would go directly to the programming and requisite supplies for events like the annual GSA prom.

Now, I wish I could say this mini-Meerkat-marathon we staged solved all of GSA Hawaii's problems.

The reality was, it didn't. But through the kindness and generosity of his heart, funding was somehow the last thing on Kaulana's mind that day. He admitted so much, that even without a dime of funding, he was not going to quit on the youths around the state that needed him.

If we didn't raise a single dime that day – and actually, I'm not sure if we did or not – I knew I was leaving there knowing that I had done absolutely everything I could to try to make a difference.

And so as we shut it down for the day, and I headed back to my hostel, I realized I'd spent a couple hours with one of the most genuine souls in the state.

My time in Hawaii wasn't limited to the GSA, either – I'd spent the morning meeting with Jill Matro of Big Brothers Big Sisters of Hawaii. She even insisted on taking me to Niko's for lunch, where I had the most delicious meal of my summer – ahi poke salad, fresh from Pier 38. (Thank you, again, Jill!)

It was a day that truly made my entire trip worth it – but after a couple of days of relaxation, a strenuous Eastbound schedule lay ahead.

NEXT STOP: Seattle

- - - - -

Kaulana Chang (14:01)

SnapChat Interview (1:50)

Jill Matro (11:24)

SnapChat Interview (1:53)

22: INSPIRE YOUTH PROJECT

"Love love love love. People we are made for love. Love each other as ourselves, for we are one!"

July 1, 2015 (State #22/50)

SEATTLE – This is where it starts getting good.

With Alaska and Hawaii now in the rear-view mirror, my eastward quest back to South Carolina was officially underway.

Fifty states in 100 days works out to two days per state, but whatever genius made the schedule (hint: me) decided it might be fun to spend a couple extra days in Hawaii.

As fun as it was to hang out in Honolulu, I'd essentially painted myself in a corner against the upcoming July 4 holiday – and, for some reason, I chose to make a visit in Seattle the morning after my flight back, rather than squeezing it in before.

Exacerbating the logistical concerns was a brutal – and I mean BRUTAL – sunburn I'd acquired on Waikiki Beach. (#TeamStrub tip No. A-1-A: Never go out in Honolulu without suntan lotion. Ever.)

Tired, red-faced but energized as ever, I made my way to the Inspire Youth Project in downtown Seattle. I'd had an unusually difficult time finding a youth organization to work with in Seattle, but when I met then-Executive Director Anh Vo, I immediately fell right back into my comfort zone.

Visiting IYP was particularly special because of the youths they serve: primarily children and teens affected in some way by HIV/AIDS and/or childhood trauma.

Because of the nature of the program, I wouldn't have a chance to meet and work with any of the youths, but I was able to offer my help by sorting through a couple of plastic crates stuffed with supplies for the upcoming summer camp program.

I re-organized toothbrushes, deodorant, shampoo and other

assorted toiletries left over from last year's camp into large, clear plastic bags – and used Meerkat to invite the world to spend a few minutes along with me.

Interviewing Anh was quite an experience. The vivid red walls of her office provided an almost-intimidating backdrop, and Anh's perfectionist tendencies meant every detail needed to be in line before we pressed record.

Throughout the summer, the visits with the kids were always the most exciting, but I enjoyed my time at IYP. You could sense a unique energy level in the room, as Anh spoke of the life-changing conversations and activities that had taken place at the table I was working on.

I was glad to be back on the mainland, relieved that one of the trickiest cities to line up had come together nicely – and excited that, for the most part, the hardest portion of the trip was history.

But as the midway point of the trip approached, I still had some massive ground to cover. After a tasty Thai lunch with the staff, I was right back on the road, heading back east and inching ever closer to achieving my lofty goal.

NEXT STOP: Missoula, Mont.

- - - - -

Anh Vo (12:43)

SnapChat Interview (1:37)

23: NCBI

"Be excellent to each other."

July 3, 2015 (State #23/50)

MISSOULA – Lengthy road trips were no big deal for the team at NCBI Missoula.

It was the beginning of a holiday weekend, celebrating the birth of the greatest country in the world, and so I was flattered that Kim Spurzem and Heidi Wallace were willing to call in the kids for a morning of fun.

I'd had to hustle from Seattle to Missoula to get this visit in, but as soon as I met the group of young people, I immediately knew I was in for one of my favorite and most memorable visits of the summer.

The group was very comfortable and conversational, because they often traveled across the traditionally red state to put on seminars about LGBT issues for other organizations and schools.

Cody, Shay, Jessica, Ingrid and Delanie were happy to meet me, but understandably even more excited to get to work on the day's project: painting the words "SAFE SPACE" in huge, capital letters on the front window.

Kim had traced the letters – several feet in size – in reverse on the big glass front windows, and set out paint palettes, sponge brushes and, perhaps most importantly, a couple boxes of donuts.

After the standard pleasantries of introductions, and a several-minute battle with the office WiFi, all that was left to do was crank the tunes and get to work.

Cody was unquestionably the "alpha male" of the group, happily and proudly leading the way as the group made rather quick work of the glass canvas. He even played the role of DJ, and, to my delight, he is just a big a Britney Spears fan as I am.

Once the WiFi situation was under control – so often, broadcasting came down to a successful signal – I fired up Meerkat and streamed the morning's activities to the world.

When the local newspaper came by to interview us, I managed to keep the live-stream going, and actually conducted the print interview live on camera. The staff photographer noticed the dichotomy of the situation and captured one of the lasting images of the trip – me proudly streaming to the world, while his lens captured the moment from behind.

By this point in the trip, I had totally found my comfort zone with the media, and even more importantly, made sure to push the staff to embrace the spotlight as well.

This is not something that every organization finds comfort in, but I felt particularly strongly about wanting Kim and Heidi to tell their stories, because I am certain that there are hurting youths out there in and around Missoula who need to know about programs like NCBI, that could change or even save their lives.

When we got around to sitting down for my own interviews, Kim and Heidi were again a bit camera-shy, but having the kids there to cheer them on really helped. We wrapped the GoPro interview, and I introduced the idea of my SnapChat interviews.

The kids were understandably hesitant to do it – not because they didn't want to, but because SnapChat journalism was clearly a new concept to them.

It was particularly interesting to interview Shay, better known as "Gay Shay [peach emoji]" on SnapChat, because she'd add me back and follow my Snaps across the rest of the country. She also shared a moment from the day on Instagram, gaining more likes than any of my photos did all summer – which reminded me that, for the next generation, these platforms are incredibly native and even more powerful than old fogies like me might realize.

As we wrapped up and I asked Kim to sign the car, she again shied away from the spotlight – squeezing NCBI's message into a tight corner on the door. My sincerest hope is that the next time NCBI Missoula, or any LGBT organization across the country, has the chance to seize the stage, they shout their message loud and proud – just like the giant multicolored letters on their own front window.

NEXT STOP: Dickinson, N.D.

- - - - -

Kim Spurzem & Heidi Wallace (11:06)

SnapChat Interview (1:53)

MISSOULIAN: Volunteer Marks Halfway Point With Stop in Missoula

24: BEST FRIENDS MENTORING PROGRAM

"Make a positive difference!"

"Life is your map to grow & give!"

July 7, 2015 (State #24/50)

DICKINSON, N.D. – My signature bright yellow T-shirt, and my South Carolina license plate, echoed the same seven letters: I AM HERE.

And although western North Dakota admittedly wasn't the most exciting spot of my trip, I was able to say "I AM HERE" for three full days, because of the way the holiday weekend had fallen.

After wrapping up with NCBI on Friday morning, I hung out at The Starving Artist coffee shop to get my video editing and photos done. I expressed interest in throwing out the first pitch for the Missoula Ospreys that night, but I didn't give enough advance notice – totally my own fault, because it was very difficult to keep planning ahead – and so I just went to the Wal-Mart parking lot for a good night's sleep.

I woke up in Missoula on July 4 and decided to do something extra American – drive across the entire state of Montana, from Missoula to Dickinson, N.D. – a 667-mile drive, significantly longer than my personal 500-mile outer limit.

But with the sun out, nothing on my schedule until Monday, and a potential extra day of rest awaiting me, I made the call – sure is nice to not have to get approval! – to head all the way across Montana.

I arrived in North Dakota around sundown, stopping first at somewhere called Chateau de Mores. The gates were open, and there is a path to the left to a house with an enormous yard. I had no idea the historical significance of Chateau de Mores, but I looked at my shirt, realized I AM HERE, and quickly realized that I had to be there for some reason.

As I sauntered back to my car, a truck full of people pulled out of the driveway, slowing down to peer at my painted car and say hi. "We're going to get some food," they said, asking me what my plans were. When I mentioned I was heading to Dickinson, they politely offered to let me stay at the house, to join them for food and fireworks.

Not knowing who these people were, I politely "accepted" their offer as they pulled away.

It was very kind of this car full of people to make such an offer, and maybe I should've stuck around and hung out at Chateau de Mores. Looking back at my trip as a whole, I have no regrets, but sometimes I do wonder how things might've played out if I didn't insist on solitude, even when there were options.

I had another half-hour or so to Dickinson, and unconfidently got back in the car and continued east. After a quick dinner stop and Meerkat stream from McDonald's, I GPS'd the neighborhood Wal-Mart, where I bought myself a six-pack of local beers, found a remote spot in the parking lot and set up camp for the night.

Without professional photo equipment, in the darkness of the night, I failed to capture the wonder of the moment – a broke young traveler, alone, with a six-pack, a makeshift bed in his backseat, silently cheers-ing the ten-plus fireworks shows going on around him. In a summertime filled with moments that were shared on every social platform imaginable, this night provided semi-private respite for a man choosing to celebrate America every day – not just July 4.

I'd spend the next two days – for some reason, I wasn't volunteering until Tuesday – hanging out at a motel. I paid for it the first night, then reached out to the CVB first thing Monday morning, who were able to connect me with a room at the same hotel for free on Monday night.

So when I got to the Best Friends Mentoring Program first thing Tuesday morning, I was totally ready to rock and roll, so to speak. I felt like I knew every inch of Dickinson, and had even completed most of my newspaper interview the day prior.

I'd made it to N.D. on Saturday night – unfortunately, just a few hours too late to either run in or volunteer for a 5K benefiting BFMP. However, all the hand-written registration forms were yet to be entered – the perfect volunteer opportunity for a quick typist like myself.

Kris Fehr, the organization's director, is a saint. You could tell she's poured her life into the program, working in a small building – well, there really aren't a lot of large buildings in Dickinson -- where, down the hall, her husband has an office as a Doctor.

It was a pleasure meeting and working with Kris and her team, and especially getting some important data entry done – allowing Kris to leverage the emails they collected on Saturday to keep in touch with race participants.

But more importantly, it was great to recharge a bit – I even went bowling – meet a wonderful staff, bring some much-needed media attention to a terrific program, and mark our nation's birthday in a way only I could imagine.

NEXT STOP: Rapid City, S.D.

- - - - -

Kris Fehr (13:54)

SnapChat Interview (1:23)

KXNET.COM: A Man Drops By Dickinson On His Mission to Volunteer in All 50 States

DICKINSON PRESS: SC Man on 100-Day Journey to Volunteer Across the Country

Best Friends Area Voices: 50 States 100 Days - Welcome to Dickinson!

25: BBBS OF THE BLACK HILLS

"A mentor empowers a person to see a possible future, and believe it can be obtained. – Shawn Hitchcock"

July 9, 2015 (State #25/50)

RAPID CITY, S.D. – For those unfamiliar with U.S. geography, Rapid City is somewhere between the "Midwest" and the "Pacific Northwest."

It's a small town – not quite as small as Dickinson, N.D., where I had just arrived from – but it's filled with lovely people, and I was lucky enough to meet one in Nicole Burdick.

Admittedly, I was amped to get to Rapid City, not just because it was finally State No. 25, but because in planning the trip, the single longest and most in-depth conversation I had with any organization was with Nicole, of Big Brothers Big Sisters of the Black Hills.

In the spring, while I was spending every free moment of every day making phone calls and sending emails, I spent over an hour chatting with, but mostly listening to, Nicole, as she explained the complexities of finding great mentors for the youths in need in South Dakota.

I didn't fully grasp the depth of Nicole's story, however, until we had a chance to meet in person at the BBBS compound.

The building itself is a sight to see, compared to many of the other Big Brothers Big Sisters facilities I'd encounter this summer. I spent about 30 minutes in the lobby, waiting for Nicole to wrap up a handful of other conversations she was wrapped up in, so I had plenty of time to admire the enormous piece of art to my right and the signed Oakland Athletics jersey (Mark Ellis** Check this) to the left.

When you enter the building, the waiting area opens up to two levels – an upstairs, lined with offices and storage space; and a downstairs, with Nicole's office, a meeting room and another large section for storage.

Nicole led us downstairs to her office, where we cruised through the standard pleasantries – "great to meet you, how's the trip going, love the office space," etc.

Most of my visits followed the same pattern – greetings, tour the facility, volunteer activity, interviews, sign the car, adios. In Rapid City, the timeframe got thrown off a bit, as Nicole and I picked up our phone conversation from the Spring and just chatted for over an hour.

As I did with most visits, I asked how Nicole had reached the Executive Director position, and her backstory blew me away. She's a born-and-raised western gal, but she'd come to Rapid City after literally throwing a dart at a map of the United States.

For someone traveling to all 50 U.S. states, who'd moved to South Carolina after weighing the pros and cons of the lower 48, hearing Nicole's background was fascinating. As she described her path to becoming Executive Director – oscillating between on- and off-the-record – I knew that Nicole's story was immensely representative of the bigger story I was discovering around the U.S.

We took a tour of the facility, which I shared with the world through Meerkat, and sat down to turn the cameras on for my interviews. As we found our seats, the local NBC affiliate showed up, a nice surprise that brought some great attention to the cause.

As the busy day wrapped up, Nicole presented me with a bag full of stuff to remember the organization by, including a coupon for a free fast-food lunch, and as quickly as the day had begun, it was over.

I only got to spend a few hours at BBBS of the Black Hills, but it was satisfying to think of all we accomplished: we gave the world a tour through live-streaming; filmed a television spot for the 5:00 news; recorded two interviews that will live on YouTube and Facebook; and, most importantly, formed a long-lasting friendship, between two people who shared a love of embracing and making the best of the unknown in this great country of ours.

NEXT STOP: Cheyenne, Wyo.

- - - - -

Nicole Burdick (11:44)

SnapChat Interview (1:20)

NEWSCENTER1.TV: Traveling Volunteer Hopes To Inspire Others in All 50 States

Wilmington, Del., Aug. 13, 2015
(Courtesy Suchat Pederson / The [Wilmington, Del.] News-Journal)

Lansing, Mich., July 25, 2015
(Courtesy Robert Killips / Lansing [Mich.] State Journal)

Missoula, Mont., July 3, 2015
(Courtesy Michael Gallacher / The [Missoula, Mt.] Missoulian)

Burlington, Vt., Aug. 3, 2015
(Courtesy Glenn Russell / Burlington [Vt.] Free Press)

"Do amazing things. Vote Abbi 2052"

July 10, 2015 (State #26/50)

CHEYENNE, Wyo. – This is, by far, the easiest state to write about.

Driving through the west was strenuous. Not that the roads were windy, nor was the weather bad, but there really just isn't much going on from Missoula to Dickinson, Dickinson to Rapid City, or Rapid City to Cheyenne.

What made this middle portion of the trip so enjoyable was the youth organizations I worked with in each spot – and none made me happier than the Boys & Girls Club of Cheyenne.

The first person I met there was Margie McLaughlin, with whom I shared one special common bond: we are both from Huntington, N.Y. In the spring, when I reached out to their organization, the call I got from Margie was filled with wonderment, almost shock – a Huntington kid was offering to come visit? Sign us up!

The second person I met there was Kalena Heil, a charming, bright-eyed blonde who played the familiar role of Swiss army knife – perfectly adaptable to every role the organization might need. She specialized in photography – a self-taught skill that translated to a full-on photography program at the Club.

While I spent most of my day with Margie and Kalena – as well as Bill Hassler, the club's Director of Operations – I was fortunate enough to cross paths with one exceptionally motivated young woman.

I introduced myself in front of the group – a chat that was lucky enough to be caught by two local television stations. (Although I never saw either story online – bummer.) As always seemed to be the case at the Boys & Girls Club, the kids were enthusiastic and very energetic, asking me all sorts of questions, especially about Hawaii.

I couldn't answer every hand that was raised, but I promised the kids I'd circle around and come visit them throughout the day. My time was limited, though, so I gathered Margie and Kalena in a meeting room, set up my GoPro and prepped them for the interview.

Knock-knock, as the door opened moments before I pressed record.

"Mr. Chris," a counselor deadpanned, "Your presence has been requested before you leave. Please don't leave without seeing Abbi."

"Sure," I replied, momentarily more concerned with snagging Margie's attention long enough to get the interviews taped.

After wrapping my interviews, I visited a few different corners of the club, including the garden, and I made my way back upstairs. "Did you talk to Abbi yet?" Margie asked.

"No," I replied, but there wasn't a chance in the world I was leaving that club without doing so.

Bill led me downstairs to look for Abbi, and when we opened the door to start looking outside, there she was – standing alone, appearing to be waiting patiently. I sat down with her at a picnic table, and felt like I'd been invited to the CEO's office.

I offered a quick introduction, and, like the truest boss you'll ever meet, Abbi cut right to it.

She wanted to speak to me, she explained, because she has really big goals, and she was in search of advice on how to achieve them.

She led with the pledge that she wants to be the first girl president, and when I reminded her that Hillary Clinton has a chance to do that, she remained steadfast that she wanted to be the first.

In addition to being the first girl president, she added, she wanted to "climb one of the highest mountains, and help people."

Now is as good a time as ever to remind you that this young woman is six years old.

She felt inspired by hearing me introduce my story, and she wanted one-on-one advice before I left.

I was holding back tears as I channeled my best advice for her – "don't ever let anyone tell you that you can't." I wasn't doing motivational speaking or anything along the way – I felt uncomfortable even introducing myself at each stop, to be honest – but this girl's self-starting, make-things-happen attitude inspired me to do some introspection and realize just how powerful an impact this trip was making.

When I passed this story back to Margie and Kalena – again, with tears in my eyes – the idea for "VOTE ABBI 2052" was hatched. For the remaining 24 states, I'd be traveling around in style, with Kalena's campaign artwork on the back of my Honda, broadcasting my favorite story of the entire summer.

NEXT STOP: Longmont, Colo.

- - - - -

Kalena Heil & Margie McLaughlin (10:40)

SnapChat Interview (1:59)

KWGN-TV: TeamStrub Volunteer Journey

27: CASA DE LA ESPARANZA

"I would rather die on my feet than live on my knees."

July 13, 2015 (State #27/50)

LONGMONT, Colo. – "I would rather die on my feet than live on my knees."

There are over 70 quotes written on my 2007 Honda Accord, but this one, written by Vanessa Escarcega at Casa de la Esparanza, sticks with me every single day.

It's a quote by Emiliano Zapata (1879-1919), a leading figure in the Mexican Revolution, and although he could have never imagined it being written on some South Carolinian's car 100 years later, his words ring especially true for me.

The quote – in English and Spanish – is painted on a wall at Casa de la Esparanza, a small facility in the heart of a housing project in the small city of Longmont.

Fate brought me to the Casa. I'd intended to volunteer in Boulder, but no one from the city ever replied to my outreach, so Longmont it was.

And I'm thankful to have made it.

Vanessa planned a terrific day of activities, starting, as usual, with a (very quick) tour of the facility, followed by cooking class.

Prior to this trip, I'd spent six months as the General Manager of Sbarro in Greenville, S.C., so chopping and preparing ingredients was right up my alley. Vanessa had gathered ingredients and recipes for two simple dishes: chicken soup, and sopapillas – pan-fried, sugary pastries.

With a photojournalist from the local paper watching, the kids – mostly bilingual, and a few exclusively Spanish-speaking – loved helping prepare the dishes. Much like E.A.T. South in Montgomery, Ala., the idea of cooking healthy food served a dual purpose – not just feeding the needy children a good meal, but instilling in them the intrinsic value of preparing a healthy dish to perpetuate a healthy lifestyle.

One of the funniest memories of the summer came when we finally got a chance to sit down and eat. (And by the way, there was something special about that soup – it was astonishingly good, for something so simple!) Vanessa – herself a bilingual young leader, with a stunning complexion – had delivered all the food to the table, and with the kids starting to devour the soup, retreated to the fridge.

"Who wants ..." she asked, and before she could even complete the simple sentence, the kids burst out of their chairs in unison.

Vanessa held up a 12-ounce bottle of hot sauce that didn't stand a chance of a long life in that fridge. I watched the kids bicker over the condiment, spilling it with reckless abandon into their bowls, with some kids definitely consuming more hot sauce than chicken broth.

Once they got their fill, the kids politely offered me the much-emptier bottle, encouraging me to try it. Meanwhile, I was quietly devouring the soup by the bowlful; I hadn't had a home-prepared meal all summer, and there was no shortage in the enormous vat the kids had helped prepare.

In fact, there was enough soup that Vanessa very kindly offered me some for the road, which made for a delicious – and more importantly, free – dinner later that night in a Wal-Mart parking lot in Nebraska.

After lunch, Vanessa tasked me with entertaining the kids while she and her intern, Sasha, cleaned up in the kitchen. I led the kids in several games of musical chairs – broadcast, of course, to the world via live-streaming – before wrapping up the day with the interview process, and getting on the road to beat the rain.

NEXT STOP: Lincoln, Neb.

- - - - -

Vanessa Escarcega (10:09)

SnapChat Interview (1:34)

LONGMONT TIMES-CALL: Cross-country Journey Brings Philanthropist to Longmont

28: LIGHTHOUSE

"Become a beacon of light for someone. Love is our change agent, education is our building block."

July 15, 2015 (State #28/50)

LINCOLN, Neb. – Lincoln is a surprisingly long drive from
Longmont, Colo.

The mileage was starting to pile up as I made my way across the so-
called "flyover states" across the western U.S.

Once I got out of Colorado, though, I could already start to sense
that success was on the horizon. Certainly at this point, there was no
"turning back" – we'd crossed the halfway point, and now all that
was really left was a wild zig-zag up into the Midwest, a quick sprint
through the Northeast, and the home stretch back to South
Carolina.

I was starting to feel weary, and so when I got word that the Lincoln
Convention & Visitors Bureau had a hotel room saved for me for
two nights, it's safe to say I was definitely feeling the Hamptonality.

I squeezed in a quick trip to meet Tracie Simpson at the CVB to say
thank you, and before I left, she walked me over towards a main
road to show me a huge, hand-painted lightbulb, complete with
inscription.

The lightbulb, it turned out, was one of 25 bulbs scattered around
the city of Lincoln – an extraordinarily complex public art project
designed to raise awareness, and inevitably funds, for Lincoln
Lighthouse.

When I reached out to Tracie, she immediately knew that Bill
Michener was the guy I'd want to connect with – and she couldn't
have been more right.

Bill Michener is the Executive Director at Lighthouse – and one of
the most well-spoken gentlemen I'd meet all summer. He was
extremely welcoming and friendly, and was happy to accommodate
my request of coming in in the morning – even though the kids

wouldn't be around until later that afternoon.

I've mentioned how I have no regrets from the trip, but I do kind of wish I had been savvy enough to plan a visit to work with the kids at Lighthouse. Bill spoke very, very highly of the content of character of all of the kids in the program – and proudly mentioned that not only is he a graduate of the Lighthouse program, but he also met his wife, Michelle, at the Lighthouse about 20 years earlier.

With no youths around, Bill left me to take a tour with Falah Al-Hirez, another very down-to-earth young man who had -- more recently than Bill, of course – graduated from Lighthous as well.

The building is rather large, with a significant basement, plus a tucked-away gymnasium that you don't really expect. The most prominent feature in the building is the first wall you see when you walk in the door – a huge wooden board, with tracks about 6 inches apart, featuring photos of all of the graduates from the last 15 years or so.

As I juggled my mobile tools – GoPro with selfie stick, iPad and, of course, iPhone – the wheels began to turn: what if this wall was completely digitized?

What if all of the tours Bill gave started and ended at a giant touchscreen, where he could summon a graduate's picture and bio just by a swipe of his finger? What if all of the stories that live in Bill's brain could be translated into a video that could not only be accessed from the screen in the building, but a matching user interface on the Lighthouse website?

It was the biggest, and probably the best, conceptual idea I'd come up with all summer, and I'm going to keep holding out hope that this idea gets in the hands of the right person at, say, Apple, or Microsoft, or some major, deep-pocketed firm that realizes how special all of the Lighthouse's stories are.

Or maybe someday, I'll have enough resources of my own to make that type of project a reality.

Who knows. But I was hopeful. I was feeling great. And I had to be, because before my next volunteer stop, I was to make a quick pitstop to run a 13.1-mile race in the heat of Okoboji, Iowa.

NEXT STOP: Des Moines

- - - - -

Bill Michener (13:49)

SnapChat Interview (1:51)

29: YESS

"#CatchDSM – Follow your passion"

"Be true to yourself. #TeamYESS #SeizeDesMoines"

July 17, 2015 (State #29/50)

DES MOINES – Sometimes, 13.1 miles are much more exhausting than 13,000.

I typically traveled directly from volunteer spot to volunteer spot, but in Iowa, I'd spend an extra night in Okoboji, to run the famed University of Okoboji Half Marathon.

The race was exhausting, both physically and emotionally. The rigor of running 13.1 miles in the summer Iowa heat is fairly obvious, but about 10 miles in, I was cruising along when a lanky young man came up from behind my left side and started high-stepping like Deion Sanders past me.

At first, I was appalled – it looked like this guy was taunting me as he was making the pass, something distance runners of any skill or experience level would never do.

My second thought was that perhaps this young man had some sort of physical disability, which was equally curious, considering the strenuous pace at which I run (I was on pace to run about 1:40 or so – nowhere near winning the race, but still very respectable).

Before my mind could process either of these reactions as fact, the kid's knees buckled and he tumbled to the ground. I immediately stopped, asked him if he was OK, and tried to flag down help, of which there was not much to be found.

I assisted as a couple racers carried the passed-out racer to the side of the road – in retrospect, he should've been moved to the other side, where there was shade – and stuck alongside the guy until help arrived.

As I crossed the finish line, I couldn't help but think about, firstly, how fortunate I have been for that never to happen to me – especially since I was in Okoboji, Iowa – and, of course, whether or not the kid was OK. I found someone who appeared to be in charge and asked him if "the kid who passed out" was alright, and he replied that he'd had upwards of 15 people pass out so far today.

Yikes.

The race was a big highlight of my summer, and followed a fun day of volunteering at YESS in Des Moines.

It was a special honor to meet some of the young people being taken care of at YESS. The beautiful, newly renovated facility was far from capacity – but a significant portion of the building remained empty due to funding levels.

It was disheartening to hear how many more youths around Des Moines were still in need of the emergency services offered there. I got to interview Kristin Huinker, the program's development manager, and it was clear she was exceptionally well prepared for a chat.

Much like Erin at Sunbeam Family Services in OKC, the high quality of the YESS facility seemed to reflect the highly professional nature, and sure-fire fundraising skills, of the staff.

Although I never saw it online, I got to do a quick television interview, and even shoot some B-roll of food prep in the kitchen (since we couldn't, obviously, portray the youths in the program). When I learned we were making chili dogs, I was wary – I spent a lot of time alone in my car – but the lunch actually turned out very good.

Overall, I was tremendously impressed with YESS, and even more honored when a personalized, hand-written thank-you card arrived in my mailbox in Greenville after I finished the trip. The smallest token of appreciation meant the world, and I hope to get the chance to go back to YESS someday to continue to help Kristin and her team spread the organization's important messages.

NEXT STOP: Rochester, Minn.

- - - - -

<u>Kristin Huinker (14:04)</u>
<u>SnapChat Interview (1:23)</u>

30: RIDEABILITY

"Your beliefs don't make you a better person … your faith in action does!"

July 19, 2015 (State #30/50)

ROCHESTER, Minn. – Jeanie Michelizzi doesn't have a grant writer.

Jeanie Michelizzi doesn't have a PR department.

Jeanie Michelizzi isn't raising millions of dollars to build an additional campus, and you're not likely to see any major celebrities making a pitch for Jeanie Michelizzi.

But the impact that Jeanie Michelizzi has had on children and families in the Rochester area is just as mighty as any of the bigger organizations I visited this summer.

RideAbility sits on a large plot of land and consists primarily of a good-sized barn, a fenced-in arena, and relatively small sensory trail.

The vision of RideAbility, as described on their site, is to provide therapeutic year-round equine activities for persons with disabilities, as well as their siblings and peers.

I was passing through on a Sunday, but Jeanie was kind enough to convene a special day of activities to show me what the program was all about.

This wasn't the first time an organization went out of its way for me – NCBI in Missoula and Girls on the Run in Boise, among others, made special arrangements, and I am still very grateful.

On this day, not only were the kids going to have some extra fun, but we were going to put the horses to work, too.

Before we got going, Jeanie gave me a tremendous introduction, and handed me a microphone that carried my voice through the arena – even though the group – a few kids, their parents, and plenty of volunteer teenagers – were gathered all around me.

The horses were all friendly and terrific, but my favorite part of the whole setup was the hot dog roller situated at the barn's end, which provided hot, fresh food for anyone who was hungry. That the barn's resident cat was situated above the roller, and was able to successfully knock a hot dog to the ground with her paw, only made the surviving dogs even more delicious.

After an intricate stretching routine, we made our way through the large, swinging gate and into the barn area. The kids and parents were all very familiar with the routine, and I was the rookie.

Delightfully, Jeanie had planned a full afternoon of activities, allowing me to experience, and share, four of the major facets of the program: the sensory trail; painting a horse; a timed race around the track; and a horse-drawn wagon ride.

Although painting a Dallas Cowboys-style star on a horse in NFC North territory was exciting, I particularly enjoyed learning the different styles of side-walking, and implementing them as we made our way through the sensory trail.

I didn't, myself, ride any of the horses – although Jeanie likely would've let me, we were running late on time, since I had to drive to Wisconsin that night – but I took immense joy in helping guide Soleil – who seemed to be everyone's favorite horse – on a trip through the sensory trail.

For those unfamiliar, a sensory trail is a path set up with a variety of objects in place to entertain and engage the horse and its rider. The sensory trail at RideAbility included bells hanging from a tree; a target to throw a ball through from the horseback; a set of stones and a sandy area, that provide different feel for the horse's hooves; and a gate that the rider can open and close (which was, by far, the trickiest of the obstacles).

It was a beautiful, sunny day, and a very eye-opening experience for a young man who was just as excited to learn from the kids as they were to hear from me.

NEXT STOP: Madison, Wis.

- - - - -

Jeanie & Jim Michelizzi (12:08)
SnapChat Interview (1:25)

31: WISCONSIN YOUTH COMPANY

"Be kind. Be curious. Follow your passion."

July 20, 2015 (State #31/50)

MADISON, Wis. – You can't stop the rain.

I already was having a fun time at Wisconsin Youth Company when confirmation came from the local news that they'd be stopping by around lunchtime.

I was sitting upstairs with Executive Director Kay Stevens, a well-spoken but modest leader who reluctantly embraced the spotlight for the day, as dozens of kids played downstairs and outside.

We were optimistic that the media would want to swing by and cover the 31st stop of my grueling, cross-country solo journey, and after a clever bit of lobbying, we turned out to be right.

Upon checking the schedule, we noticed the next activity was to bring the kids across the street to the splash park.

When the idea of joining the kids at a splash park was first floated, I was a little hesitant.

I was pretty tired, having slept the night before in the so-called #HondaHotel – the back seat of my beloved 2007 Honda Accord – and it wasn't exactly scorching hot out.

But this was a once-in-a-lifetime trip, and I quickly moved all-in – with the hope of convincing the venerable executive director sitting next to me to join me.

If I was going to get wet in the name of some solid B-roll, Kay Stevens was definitely coming with me.

We wrapped up our in-house interviews – Kay's first experience with the SnapChat platform – checked the clock, and headed back downstairs.

I headed outside to notice some gray skies slowly, ever so slowly, shimmeying towards us, and knew right then that there was an imminent chance of some trouble.

The television truck pulled up, and Kay – who was not clued in to my plan to soak the boss – broke the bad news: the kids would have to stick around WYC, due to the threat of the impending storms.

Bummer. Like Mom and Dad canceling a trip to an amusement park, you never grow out of the feeling of disappointment when the weather forces a change in your plans.

But in that moment, I came to another realization: this was, more or less, the first time that the weather had had any effect on my scheduled activities – all summer long.

Sure, it drizzled a bit in Anchorage. Yes, there was a downpour in Jacksonville – but only after I'd rallied and volleyed with the kids. Yes, there was a thunderstorm in Dickinson, N.D. – but only after I'd taken in hours of 4th of July fireworks from a Wal-Mart parking lot.

With all the entropy that goes along with visiting 50 states in 100 days, Mother Nature seemed to be looking over me all along – and, who knows, maybe she made the right move here, too. As worn-out as I was feeling in Wisconsin, exerting extra energy and getting soaking wet, when it wasn't blistering hot to dry everyone off, might well have left me under the weather and unable to push through the rest of the midwest.

As it was, in Wisconsin – and along the rest of the trip – the very first words of wisdom inscribed on my car turned out to be true:

"EWOP" – or, Everything Works Out Perfectly.

NEXT STOP: Peoria, Ill.

- - - - -

<u>Kay Stevens (13:03)</u>

<u>SnapChat Interview (1:40)</u>

"A little time makes a big difference."

July 22, 2015 (State #32/50)

PEORIA, Ill. – Volunteering with youth organizations in all 50 states, over the course of 100 days, left little time for relaxation and recreation.

I was able to grab a local beer in Lincoln, Neb., and catch up for a little bit with friends in New Orleans, but for the most part, I found myself either volunteering, video editing, driving or sleeping almost the entire way.

My one true escape was Minor League Baseball.

Knowing that I'd be in the neighborhood of tons of minor league parks all summer, I'd reached out to MiLB before the summer began, hoping to simplify, and capitalize on, the idea of traveling from park to park to throw out first pitches.

After my pitch to MiLB missed low and outside (get it? Baseball joke?), I decided to push on and contact as many individual teams as I could along the way.

The teams – especially around the Southeast – were thrilled to welcome me, and I ended up throwing out almost a dozen first pitches around the country, and plugging the individual organization I worked with in each city.

Most of the games, of course, were at night, which further complicated my hope of involving some of the kids and/or staff members at each game.

The one exception, though, was Peoria.

An 11:35 a.m. start left me precious little time to meet up with Jamie Truelove, Nicole Campen and the entire BBBS Heart of Illinois team at their office.

On short notice, Jami had received approval to swing a row full of free tickets, so that some of the youths in the program could come enjoy a game with me.

Before we could relax and enjoy the sunshine, though, I needed to be on the field to throw out the first pitch.

Early.

Not often did I find myself both driving, and parking, with purpose, but here I was, weaving between school buses to figure out some way to get myself into that ballpark before they moved on without me.

I had failed to account for the fact that the mid-morning summertime games are always filled with kids from summer camps, and so parking outside of this normally quiet stadium was a nightmare.

I swung around to a side street and saw a "parking spot" on a corner that, 99% of the time, I wouldn't even have considered. Nicole kept driving, but I knew this was my only shot. I squeezed up to the bumper behind me and literally ran into the stadium, even eschewing the will-call line with a (truthful) plea that I was late to my shot to throwing out the first pitch.

Thankfully – as it always seemed to – everything worked out just perfectly; the television crew waiting inside for me was polite and understanding, and produced one of the best news stories of my summer.

Unfortunately, the kids made it into the stadium several minutes after my first pitch, but they were so impressed to be sitting with a guy who was just on the field.

We did a live-stream from the seats, where I introduced the world to Felix, a sharp-minded young soccer player in need of a big. I even had a chance to bring Felix over to the Chiefs mascot, a magical moment that never gets old.

When the day wound down, I sincerely thanked Nicole and Jami for making this terrific day possible. It was another very memorable afternoon in a summer overflowing with magic.

NEXT STOP: Indianapolis

- - - - -

Jami Truelove & Nicole Campen (10:13)

SnapChat Interview (1:45)

PEORIA JOURNAL: New Yorker will Throw Out First Pitch at Chiefs Game

CENTRALILLINOISPROUD.COM: Helping Kids: 50 States in 100 Days

33: FREEWHEELIN' COMMUNITY BIKES

"Spread the freewheel! <3"

July 23, 2015 (State #33/50)

INDIANAPOLIS – I've never loved riding bikes.

Part of it stems back to a "traumatic" experience I had as a kid, where a rogue shoelace got caught in my bike's spokes, leading to a pretty nasty gash on my leg.

Perhaps part of it is because of my love of running.

Whatever the reason, I was tremendously relieved when I met Jennifer Cvar, of Freewheelin' Community Bikes in Indianapolis, that she hadn't planned some mini-Tour de France around the neighborhood.

It was reminiscent of a pattern that was becoming increasingly commonplace throughout the summer: I was almost always a little nervous and unsure about what an organization might have in store.

I'm certain the organizations felt the same way about me – a shaggy-haired drifter in a painted car, equipped with a GoPro, a bottle of water and not much else – but their trepidation always seemed to melt away the moment we met.

It was a repetitive but important exercise, state after state, as I was able to wash away my own misconceptions about each organization – and, through social and traditional media, hopefully help do the same in each community.

Jennifer arrived a couple minutes after I did to open up the shop – a small storefront, piled high with bikes and bike parts, with a big storage area located in the back.

We were soon joined by Roger, a tall, thin, bearded fellow who couldn't appear to be more in his element. He was friendly but focused, even insisting on continuing to work while I filmed 10-second sound bites for my SnapChat interviews. I found a passion point by asking him about the Tour de France, which he was passively listening to through a live-stream on a nearby computer.

Save, possibly, for other media types, it was very possible that I knew less about bikes and bike mechanics than anyone else who'd ever been in that back section of the shop.

Jennifer patiently took it in stride, noticing that I wanted to help any way I could, but all I was really doing was sort of getting in Roger's way.

I was invited to meet a class of bike-loving kids, but they wouldn't be arriving until the early afternoon. Having missed a great opportunity in Nebraska, I volunteered to stick around and see what the kids would be up to.

Jennifer gathered some cleaning supplies, and I did what any totally clueless volunteer would be able to do — sweep, vacuum and wipe down dirty surfaces. It definitely felt nice to make a difference, even in such a small way, with an organization that wouldn't ordinarily be among my core interests.

It wasn't until Jen brought us around to the back that I truly gained an appreciation for how the organization helped Indy's kids. There were robes hanging from the ends of rows of shelves, and the different colors signified the hierarchy of skill levels in bike maintenance.

When children sign up for programming at FCB, they are assigned a bike, and while riding is certainly the goal, it is looked at not as a right, but as a privilege to be earned.

Much like the Malivai Washington Youth Foundation in Jacksonville is about tennis, but not really about tennis; and Girls on the Run is about running, but not really about running; FCB is about bikes, but it's not really about bikes.

Instead, it uses the two-wheeled vehicle as a vehicle for learning important life skills throughout adolescence. Jennifer, her staff and volunteers take infinitely more pride in watching the youths develop those skills, than thinking about who might be the next big Indianapolis professional cyclist.

It was an eye-opening day in one of America's coolest cities – a town I'd love to have some more time to explore. But my time was short, and a totally new experience awaited just across the state line.

NEXT STOP: Lansing, Mich.

- - - - -

Jennifer Cvar (9:10)

SnapChat Interview (1:50)

34: IMPRESSIONS

"Volunteer is a good line on your resume."

July 25, 2015 (State #34/50)

LANSING, Mich. – "I'm a big floss guy."

It's true, I do appreciate the importance of dental hygiene – but even with the seemingly random set of activities I'd be tasked with all summer long, I never imagined hauling an enormous toothbrush around a gigantic set of fake teeth.

The set is just a small part of what makes Impression 5 such an exciting place for kids and their families to spend quality time in downtown Lansing.

And though I doubt they'll write "I'm a big floss guy" on my gravestone someday, it was a perfectly colorful observation by Judy Putnam, the newspaper columnist tasked with documenting my fun times in Michigan.

Impression 5 Science Center was certainly unlike any other nonprofit I visited this summer. The building's upper floor is chock full of science-centered stations, designed to delight each of your five senses – thus, the name "Impression 5."

As was typically the case, my day began early – in fact, before the center even opened up.

After an adventurous attempt at parking – the amorphous lot layout at Impression 5 could easily qualify as a multi-sensory exhibit of its own – I finally got inside to meet Marilyn Doty Larson, the organization's venerable volunteer coordinator.

In the weeks leading up to my visit, Marilyn had been as friendly and communicative as any other coordinator I'd been in contact with all summer. She'd gone out of her way to arrange for a hotel room for me to stay at, complete with stellar WiFi and even a kitchenette.

Marilyn had even floated the idea of dispatching me out to a community golf tournament, where Impression 5's Executive Director was playing that day. I'd quietly crossed my fingers – how cool would that be? – but when the idea was shot down, I was still pretty stoked for a fun day at this innovative facility.

What I hadn't realized before I began conversing with Marilyn was that that Executive Director – Erik Larson – is her son. Interestingly, Marilyn had served as the volunteer coordinator years ago, and had set out for retirement, before her son convinced her to come back and reprise her role.

As such, Marilyn – a vocal Michigan State fan, of course – had a great handle on all the ins and outs of the facility, as well as the precise volunteer staffing levels needed to steer the ship smoothly.

Marilyn's years of experience also seemingly gave her the inside track on securing superstar volunteers. Mary Beth Fletcher, the former science lab coordinator at a local elementary school, had come by on an "off day" to give me a quick tour of all the excitement upstairs.

Of all the volunteers I met this summer, Mary Beth was the most "qualified" for the position – and I don't think it was close. She wasn't just there to wipe down the devices, or straighten out piles of blocks – Mary Beth's explanations and insights made it seem like she could've designed each machine.

I got to circle around the exhibits twice – once with Mary Beth, and then again with Marilyn, once the local newspaper arrived, when I so suavely demonstrated my love passion for dentistry.

I even got to participate in one of the center's signature activities – making a plastic bag of "slime," from household kitchen ingredients. When I learned we could take our slime home with us, I wondered if anyone had ever transported slime across 15 state lines in the middle of the summer. (Turns out, it held up OK!)

All in all, Impression 5 was an exciting change of pace from many of the summer camp-like activities I'd encountered, and it's certainly a great asset to the city of Lansing. More than any other spot I visited, Impression 5 would certainly benefit from leveraging interactive social media platforms, and I was excited to at least have opened their eyes to the possibilities of exposure to a national audience.

NEXT STOP: Toledo, Ohio

- - - - -

Marilyn Doty Larson (12:08)

SnapChat Interview (1:49)

LANSING STATE-JOURNAL: Trailblazer Hits 50 States in 100 Days

"When you can read, you can succeed. <3 Chris, thank you for giving back so that others succeed."

July 26, 2015 (State #35/50)

TOLEDO, Ohio – Sometimes, the unexpected turns are the most fun.

I'd arrived in Toledo to meet Jeanette Hrovatich, Executive Director of Read For Literacy.

From the moment we began talking, I knew Jeanette was a big-picture thinker. Her passion for teaching children to read was rooted much deeper than just hoping to improve grades in Toledo's English classes; her logic, as she'd write on my car, was that "If you can read, you can succeed."

And so while she clearly enjoyed speaking about the ins and outs of the Read for Literacy program, Jeanette hoped to swing my first-ever visit to Toledo to a broader view of the issues and solutions native to the city.

First things first, though: there was work to be done. Jeanette had collected around 100 children's books, and our primary goal on this sunny Sunday afternoon was to swing by a local shelter to deliver them, along with several boxes of donuts for good measure.

I was sitting shotgun in Jeanette's hatchback for a guided tour of the city, starting with a stop at a local donut shop.

The store manager behind the glass seemed pleasantly surprised when we inquired about buying (almost) every pastry left in the building. On a Sunday, it seemed, almost everyone in town made their donut run before church, which meant once we cleaned the place out, it'd be a nice, easy early close for the staff.

We transported the haul to Family House, a spot I figured Jeanette's organization frequented. As it turned out, this was Read For Literacy's first visit there, and I intended to make it a memorable one.

As I pulled the books out of the rolling crate and spread them on a long table, I sifted through the stack looking for familiar titles.

I settled on "Where The Wild Things Are," and Jeanette saw my eyes light up.

I was honored to have a few minutes to read to the group of kids and parents, both of whom happily collected the books – and donuts.

It was a special few minutes for me, not just getting to read to the group, but having the chance to interact directly with a couple of the young people as they decided on what they'd be reading next.

As was often the case this summer – much like with Abbi in Cheyenne – one of my favorite moments of the day came off-camera. After I read Maurice Sendak's classic, I took it over to a young boy and offered it to him, if he promised me he'd read it again on his own.

Deal.

As quickly as the moment came, it was gone. Jeanette and I had to go, as we were hoping to meet up with Steve North, of Lifeline Toledo.

This gentleman was fascinating. We decided on a local coffee shop, where I had fresh squeezed grapefruit juice – and take my word for it, when you're 35 states into a 50-state road trip, fresh squeezed juice of any kind is a godsend – and we shared stories.

Steve and I clicked pretty well – he seemed interested in my cross-country quest, while I was impressed by the two major feathers in his cap: LifeLine Toledo, and 4.5 Poverty Immersion.

In short: LifeLine Toledo is a completely revamped school bus,

155

offering one day a week of free, no-strings-attached health care, featuring doctors and nurses who volunteer their time; 4.5 Poverty Immersion is a 4 ½-day experience, led by Steve, that closely simulates the real-life struggles of living on the streets of Ohio.

Certainly, I could've spent a whole day – if not 4.5 immersive days – just with Steve, but our collective time was short – as is the word count in this column. As quickly as the day had begun, Jeanette bid me farewell – and I was eastbound again, into my journey's final stretch.

NEXT STOP: Pittsburgh

- - - - -

Jeanette Hrovatich & Steve North (16:43)

SnapChat Interview (1:50)

156

"Don't stop believin'!"

"Take the time to enjoy nature. (Go hug a tree!)"

July 28, 2015 (State #36/50)

PITTSBURGH – I wasn't expecting the bush honeysuckle to put up
such a fight.

It was a sunny, humid evening at Frick Park, the largest park in
Pittsburgh, and I had a rough idea of our task going in: remove as
much of the invasive honeysuckle as possible.

It was my second day in Pittsburgh, after a much-needed day of
work and evening of rest, including a great dinner and couple of
beers with Steve Sasman of the Million Dollar Tesla Trip.

I'd learned of Steve while watching a Meerkat stream in Wichita,
Kan. Steve and I were on similar but different solo journeys – I, of
course, was visiting 50 states in 100 days, working with youth
nonprofits; Steve was visiting 48 states, and Canada, over an
indeterminate number of days, interviewing as many people with
interesting stories as possible.

We didn't think our paths would cross – bummer – but then I got a
phone call from Steve somewhere around Illinois, letting me know a
meet-up would indeed be possible.

I took a spin with Steve on my first night in Pittsburgh, letting him
know the true value of my visit would be day No. 2 – when I'd head
to the Pittsburgh Parks Conservancy to roll up my sleeves and get
some work done.

And so when Steve accepted my invite to join for a night of
volunteering, neither one of us realized how taxing this work would
actually be.

We were led by a handful of parks employees, including Lauryn
Statler, the online engagement coordinator, whom I'd interviewed
earlier in the day, and joined by a half-dozen or so camera-shy kids
in their late teens, perhaps early 20's.

When we arrived at the designated spot deep in the park, staffer Rosie Wise unloaded the truck, including a heavy-duty, metal orange jack that dwarfed your average garden scissors.

She asked the group who was up to the task, and, feeling as energized as ever, I eagerly raised my hand. I lived by the mantra "Go big or go home," especially in the Steel City, and I was determined to make the most of my limited time in battle.

And boy, were the weeds up for the challenge. I trudged the metal contraption up the hill and immediately realized the scope of what we were facing: copious amounts of bush honeysuckle, some fleeting, and some very deep-rooted.

As a horticulture novice, I initially had some difficulty identifying which roots were "bad" and which ones were OK. Rosie and the staff were happy to help point out the problems – and I brought the muscle.

If you know me personally, or have seen a live-stream of mine, you know I'm far from the strongest guy around. In fact, I'm fairly diminutive, and a lack of exercise combined with a steady diet of Bob Evans and Schlotzky's hadn't done much for my core strength.

But I have heart. I have determination. And on this day, I even had an eager-minded road-tripping buddy – the L.C. Greenwood to my Mean Joe Greene, if you will – and we were ready to conquer.

The live-stream I did from Frick Park that day must've been comical to watch. The goal of my equipment was to use leverage to literally uproot these plants – often easier said than done.

I found myself grimacing, jumping, squeezing – even, at points, being suspended in mid-air, trying to use every ounce of my might to make progress on these deep-seated problems.

When Rosie and the crew said our time was up, I was disappointed: together, we'd made quite a bit of progress, but all I could focus on was the vast forest that lay beyond, still filled with bush honeysuckle.

Steve and I were both starving – turns out, tearing up roots builds an appetite – so after a satisfying trip to Qdoba, I gave some more thought to how our day had gone, and I came to an important realization.

We didn't clear out all the bush honeysuckle – far from it, in fact. But we went in with our heads down and, in the time that we had, gave it absolutely everything we had, and then some. We might not have fixed all the problems in the forest, but we walked out knowing that we'd made a difference in that moment.

In many ways, I thought, it felt like a metaphor for my entire trip: I might not have solved all the world's problems, but by showing up and giving it everything I had, I helped solve some of them.

And hopefully, I remembered, my efforts might inspire others to give it their all, too.

NEXT STOP: Binghamton, N.Y.

- - - - -

Lauryn Statler (10:55)

SnapChat Interview (1:39)

BONUS SNAPCHAT: Steve Sasman, Million Dollar Tesla Trip (1:31)

SUPERCHARGED SHOW: Chris Strub

37: MAGIC PAINTBRUSH PROJECT

"Be Maddie Strong!"

"Believe in magic!"

"You cannot steer a ship from the front."

July 30, 2015 (State #37/50)

BINGHAMTON, N.Y. – This is where the emotions really started to kick in.

I first visited Binghamton in the summer of 2003, to prepare for my freshman year of college at SUNY Binghamton that fall. Save for the undergrad summers at home, I'd spend the next 11 years living in the Southern Tier – four on campus, and the ensuing seven in the heart of the city's downtown.

In 2014, my first trip around the United States began and ended in Binghamton – a quaint college town perhaps known best for Spiedies, the 2014 Eastern League Champion B-Mets, and my alma mater.

So after circling through 36 states, it was understandably overwhelming to come "home" – even if just for a couple days.

I'd planned the trip around two key dates: first, the Kona Half Marathon in Hawaii – which I ended up not running for financial reasons – and the Binghamton University Alumni Golf Tournament, which I got to attend on Friday. I've always felt very compelled to support my alma mater in any way possible, and I was thrilled to spend one of my 100 days on the road at the Links at Hiawatha Landing with scores of fellow Bearcats.

But after a couple fun days in Pittsburgh, my first priority was to spend time with the Magic Paintbrush Project. As I admitted to Jen O'Brien, the Executive Director, in our YouTube interview, the MPP was the only organization I knew 100% that I wanted to work with from the moment I started planning my trip.

I was at the Holiday Inn in downtown Binghamton trading text messages with Jen when I realized how special a day we were in for. Jen, one of the busiest women you'll ever meet, was crushed up against several project deadlines, but had gone out of her way to plan a special event for kids from Horace Mann Elementary School, at Recreation Park.

With a threat of rain looming – it was Binghamton, after all – Jen decided to slide the event across the street, to a covered outdoor area just outside of the school.

As she and her staff worked quickly to unpack supplies from her car, I insisted on a much-needed hug – a hug that might not have seemed tremendously significant at the moment, but meant absolutely everything to me.

Unlike all the other connections I'd made so far during the summer, this hug was years in the making. It was four years ago, at that same Binghamton University Alumni golf tournament, that Jen O'Brien had a brief conversation with me that absolutely stuck in my head.

I was working for Ad Elements, a Binghamton-based advertising agency, at the time, and Jen had heard of the results I was producing through social media for our clients.

She came over to me, looked me squarely, but politely, in the eye, and asked if I could take a closer look at what she was doing with the Magic Paintbrush Project – the cause most near and dear to her heart.

Little did she know that that brief conversation would stick with me for years – and likely for the rest of my life.

As Jen addressed the kids and offered them instruction on how the day's painting project would go, I stood by and admired the scope of what she's been able to accomplish – taking MPP to a regional level, and helping thousands of children learn important life skills through the colorful power of paint.

The visit was a total blur. Four television stations – and, notably, not the local newspaper, where I'd worked for six years – came by, and I spent almost the entire time giving interviews. By the time all the media left, the delighted kids were wrapping up – I hardly had a moment to chat with them at all.

I even had the opportunity to meet up with Amy Shaw, from the Chamber of Commerce, and more importantly, mother of Maddie Shaw – the young girl whose courageous battle against Ewing's Sarcoma was a constant motivation for me to keep going.

The day, my whole stay in Binghamton – heck, the trip in general, for the most part – was a blur. But it was a magical blur, a life-changing blur, and, I hoped, a world-changing blur. And even if it wasn't, I could sleep knowing that I'd done everything I could to try.

Speaking of sleep, there was little rest for the weary – after a long weekend in my old hometown, I was off to Vermont – and another long night in the #HondaHotel.

NEXT STOP: Burlington, Vt.

- - - - -

Jen O'Brien (11:24)

SnapChat Interview (1:20)

BINGHAMTONHOMEPAGE.COM: BU Alumnus Visits 50 States in 100 Days

WBNG: Students Paint with a Special Guest on a Mission

"Follow your dreams!"

Aug. 2, 2015 (State #38/50)

BURLINGTON, Vt. – Six states in seven days.

If there was a one-week stretch of my trip that was going to break me, it would be this one: six states, six youth organizations, in seven days.

I'd had a little time to recharge in Binghamton, but a lot of that freshness in your legs goes out the window when you sleep in your car – which I did during my first night in Burlington.

By traveling to Vermont on Saturday, I gave myself a full day on Sunday -- theoretically to explore the beauty of one of the Northeast's prettiest cities.

Instead, I spent all day sitting at a Panera, mostly writing emails, trying to tie up the loose ends that still awaited during this kamikaze volunteerism stretch.

I obviously had Vermont lined up, plus New Hampshire and Maine, but still needed confirmation on Massachusetts and Rhode Island, and I was totally clueless in Connecticut. Even if I got all of them lined up, I still had vacancies ahead in Maryland and West Virginia, or was that Virginia proper …

It was a mess. A whirlwind. An astonishing amount of preparation before the trip still wasn't nearly enough, and it was all beginning to weigh on me a bit.

One of my friends decided this would be a good time to recommend that I "hire somebody" to help, which wasn't tremendously comforting after I'd slept in the back seat of my Honda Accord the night before. I was definitively, painfully broke by this point – but there was obviously no turning back.

I managed to get my laundry done at the King St. Laundromat, an act whose symbolism I wouldn't recognize until after I met Gabe Tufo Strouse at King Street Center – literally a block away.

Burlington's not a terribly large city, and so as Gabe explained to me, there are large, drastic divisions of socioeconomic status in relatively close quarters. King Street Center is a stone's throw from the heart of downtown; another stone's throw from the water; and similarly close to some of the more economically challenged sections of the town.

Burlington is also a town filled with transplants from other countries, and it was a delight to meet a handful of non-native youths in a classroom setting upstairs at the center.

We were joined by a television station and the Burlington Free Press, which meant it was again my turn to address the youths in the room.

Speaking to a group of young children can be tough. Speaking to a group of young children who have no idea who you are can be even tougher.

And speaking to a group of young children, who have no idea who you are, while you're on TV, in an unfamiliar city, while 12 weeks into a solo, unsponsored, 50-state quest, is, well, you get the idea.

I wish I'd had the foresight to prepare a speech, or bring along some fun props, or a jack-o-lantern of chocolate, or something that would've been more broadly entertaining to the kids – not just in Burlington, but in every city where I was encouraged to speak. (The stage would get even scarier in New Jersey ...).

I lived the trip with no regrets, though, and I hope the day was still a memorable one for the youths in the program.

Saying farewell to the folks in Burlington was tricky. The media followed me and Gabe out to my car, where she found a corner to sign – the car was definitely filling up by now. As was often the case,

I felt like I wish I could do more, but the clock was ticking – and a whole lot of great kids – plus one troublemaker – awaited in New Hampshire.

NEXT STOP: Concord, N.H.

- - - - -

Gabe Tufo Strouse (12:52)

SnapChat Interview (1:39)

WCAX: Young traveler visits Vermont nonprofit to inspire volunteers

BURLINGTON FREE PRESS: 50-state Volunteer Stops in Burlington

39: BGC OF CENTRAL NEW HAMPSHIRE

"Just go for it!"

Aug. 4, 2015 (State #39/50)

CONCORD, N.H. – This time, I was ready.

I loved visiting different chapters of the Boys & Girls Club across the United States, because the kids at every chapter were consistently enthusiastic about the program.

At my last stop at a BGC, in Cheyenne, Wyo., I was perplexed when the staff essentially handed me off to a pair of kids to take a tour.

Little did I realize that it would be one of the most fun and eye-opening experiences of the whole trip, in addition to giving me more of a chance to chat with and get to know the kids.

So after a quick tour of the facility – and short aside to find the WiFi password, of course – with Club Director Bob Carter, I was 100% ready when he more or less handed me off to a young girl named Destiny.

Destiny seemed to know everything about the club – and, seemingly, everyone in it. Every question I asked, she had a sharp answer, and even as she introduced me to her friends and counselors, it seemed her biggest concern was that I was having fun along the way.

Little did she realize, of course, that hanging around one of the top chapters of the Boys & Girls Club in the country, and having an opportunity to tell their story to the world, was about the most fun I could be having on this beautiful, sunny day.

As the morning continued on, the kids splintered off in the upstairs room into small groups, each focusing on a favorite game or activity. After hanging for a minute with two young boys obsessed with small toy cars, I found a seat at a table to play cards.

With almost full freedom to take pictures and live-stream – about five or six kids had to wear "pinnies" to show they couldn't be photographed, which most of them did not seem to appreciate – I fired up Meerkat and broadcast my first-ever game of Spit, against a very competitive youth who was more excited to explain the game than to compete.

That friendly spirit was pervasive through 99% of my visit – almost every single kid at the Club was eager to explain what they were up to, excited to show me what they were doing, and make me feel like part of the activity.

All, of course, except for one youth, whose name I don't remember, possibly because he never told me.

As Destiny brought me outside, where groups of kids were divided into playing basketball, goofing around on the soccer field and drawing with sidewalk chalk, I more focused on what was taking place in front of me, than what might lurk behind.

And, out of nowhere, as if we were flashing back to 1992, when I would've been right there with the kids – off came my hat.

I was in disbelief. With no winds in the air, this was a dastardly playground act if there ever was one.

I whirled around to see my hat in the grasp of a grinning youth. "I've got your hat!" he cackled, and I cringed as he tossed it up towards the rim of the nearby basketball hoop.

My gray Binghamton Bearcats cap might not seem like a big deal, but I'd worn it in every picture, in every state, so far – and I wasn't thrilled that it'd been swiped.

I watched helplessly as my hat fluttered into a muddy, shallow puddle just behind the hoop, and I snatched it up from the murk before the bully could inflict further damage.

Destiny and I rolled our eyes and laughed, and moments later, the counselors reconvened all the kids to head inside for the next activity. With my interviews with Club Director Chris Emond in the books, and no sign of the local media, it seemed as good a time as ever to hit the road.

NEXT STOP: Portland, Maine

- - - - -

Chris Emond (8:23)

SnapChat Interview (1:52)

"Think BIG and dream BIG!"

"Be the change."

Aug. 5, 2015 (State #40/50)

PORTLAND, Maine – I dug my toes into the sand, closed my eyes and took a deep breath as the ocean climbed up my feet.

It felt like just yesterday that I'd done the exact same thing on Waikiki Beach, before heading to visit with Big Brothers Big Sisters of Honolulu.

It was remarkable to reflect on the fact that these two organizations, which couldn't geographically be much further apart, shared the same mission and values – and were simultaneously helping youths in their respective parts of the country strive for their own goals and dreams.

And here I was – alone, as usual – deeply inhaling the crisp summertime Maine air, trying as hard as I could to fully appreciate what would surely be the most serene moment remaining on my journey.

I love York Beach. The town played an enormous part in my first quest around the United States, during the summer of 2014, when I spent a couple days at my Aunt & Uncle's cabin. After that trip ended, I retreated to the cabin for several weeks of genuine solitude – time that was spent mostly physically editing videos, but mentally assessing whether or not a second, more meaningful journey would be on the horizon.

And now here I was, about 80% done with my second trip – financially destroyed, but emotionally 100% satisfied.

There was still work to be done, obviously, but after flights to Alaska and Hawaii, Herculean day trips across Montana and a mental meltdown in New Mexico, I was as prepared as could be for the final stretch through New England and back down to South Carolina.

I'd slipped a day off into my six-state-in-seven-days sprint, which ended up filled with back-to-back-to-back-to-back phone conversations from a Starbucks parking lot about Huntington and Baltimore.

I also squeezed in dinner at a nearby Applebee's, where I met Lauren, aka "PuffLikesBeer," the restaurant's manager and a fellow live-streamer who was greatly entertained that I was Meerkat-ing my dinner with Vincenzo Landino and dozens of other socially savvy viewers.

But as cathartic as my time in Portland was, I was amped to fire it up for the young team at Big Brothers Big Sisters of Southern Maine.

I stopped by on my "off day" to get done my two interviews with Executive Director Dave Perron and Director of Development Casey Hartford, which freed us up on Thursday to focus on a great idea Casey had pitched: a "man on the street"-type exercise, where we'd walk around with cameras to gauge the community's awareness of the program.

This was a terrific concept, one that became an inside joke amongst their staff as they yielded credit for who had originally come up with it. Regardless of its origin, Casey and I, along with Program Manager Lindsay Hart, headed out for the morning for a (very) long walk.

Paralleling the entirety of my trip, the idea of exploring was informative, eye-opening and exciting, if not complicated a bit by the cameras. We struck up a conversation with a guy sitting with an unbelievably adorable dog, only to learn the owner would decline to be on camera. (Didn't stop me from getting a picture with said dog.)

As we found ourselves talking to mostly men, Lindsay talked me into heading over and sitting on a bench alongside a professional young woman on a lunch break, which went about as well as every other time I've ever tried to talk with a professional young woman: terribly.

The shyness of those two aside, the day actually went fairly well, as we came across quite a few people happy to learn more about Big Brothers Big Sisters. One twenty-something young man in particular, sitting alone at the park with a book, was delighted to chat with us, on the record, about the program, and even expressed interest not only becoming a big, but encouraging his friends to join with him.

As most of my Northeast visits went, it was a bit of a blur – and with no more rest days penciled in, it was time to hit the road. Driving south into Massachusetts would be my inevitable return to soul-crushing traffic – and I had a very big day at Camp Massapoag on the horizon.

NEXT STOP: Lowell, Mass.

- - - - -

David Perron & Casey Hartford (13:42)

SnapChat Interview (1:47)

41: GREATER LOWELL YMCA

"M-A-SSA-PO-A-G spells Massapoag, Massapoag. That's the place we go to in the summer, summer. That's the place we meet new comers, comers. M-A-SSA-PO-A-G, you see, that's the place where no blame or no shame can be, connected with MASSAPOAG for me! Yipee!"

"Always have hope! - Moira, Hope for Creativity"

Aug. 5, 2015 (State #41/50)

DUNSTABLE, Mass. – It's never bad to feel like a kid again.

It was a gorgeous, warm summer day at Camp Massapoag in rural Dunstable, about a 20-minute drive from Lowell, where I'd slept very comfortably the night before.

The city of Lowell had very kindly put me up at the UMass-Lowell Inn & Conference Center, home of perhaps the most comfortable bed I'd come across all summer. (Although you could absolutely make a case for the Marriott Wakiki Beach, or even the exquisite guest room at the home of Liz Ellerson in Montgomery, Ala.)

The main facility for the Lowell YMCA was less than a mile from the conference center, which seemed almost too simple for a trip that was built off of complex travel and lodging arrangements.

If you've never driven in Massachusetts before, you should know, too, that even a one-mile trek typically involves windy, circuitous twists and turns, multi-stoplight intersections and tricky parking situation.

And so when I rolled up to the main facility of the YMCA about 5 minutes late, and my phone rang with a Massachusetts area code, I knew something had to be amiss.

It was Director of Operations Kevin Morrissey, informing me that I was, in fact, at the wrong spot.

Back into the driver's seat I went, and I made my way to rural Dunstable, home of the iconic Camp Massapoag.

It was there that I'd meet dozens of great people, including Morrissey, Chief Executive Officer Ray Adams – and scores of cool kids, some even equipped with water balloons.

And if I can offer one piece of advice, make it this: if you're ever 41 states in a 50-state philanthropic road trip, and a sixth-grader hands you a water balloon with the gregarious, friendly CEO within range, and the Club Director quietly egging you on – don't miss.

Thankfully, I didn't – in a moment we were even able to capture on SnapChat, and share with the world.

For a few seconds, it was great to feel like a kid again, exploding a water balloon over the unsuspecting head of a well-respected CEO, and helping everyone to remember that it's OK to have fun sometimes.

Ray and Kevin were such good sports on this day, very graciously leading me around to all corners of the facility and accommodating my interview requests with ease. Ray taught me the ins and outs of "Gaga," a fast-paced, high-intensity game in a wooden octagon that I was simply terrible at. Kevin offered me the opportunity to shoot a bow and arrow for the first time, which didn't actually go quite as badly as you might expect.

I even considered jumping in the lake, the signature feature at Camp Massapoag, which undoubtedly would've been fun but also would've complicated the logistics of safely – and dryly – heading west, into Rhode Island.

I spent a good portion of the morning chatting with Melissa Hanson of the Lowell Sun, a bright-eyed, leggy reporter whom I didn't mind sitting with for a bit longer than the average interview. She and her photographer did a terrific job with a story, with accompanying video, and it was a joy to dive a bit into my personal history as a YMCA camper growing up myself.

It was a jam-packed day to highlight a jam-packed week, and I was far from done. After another round of difficult good-byes and the standard photo ops, I was right back on the road for the short trip to Providence.

NEXT STOP: Providence, R.I.

- - - - -

<u>Ray Adams & Kevin Morrissey (11:50)</u>

<u>SnapChat Interview (1:55)</u>

<u>LOWELL SUN: Former YMCA Camper Giving Back, One State at a Time</u>

42: YOUTH BUILD PROVIDENCE

"Enter to learn, depart to serve."

Aug. 8, 2015 (State #42/50)

PROVIDENCE, R.I. – After months of tackling states like Texas, California and Montana, it was finally time to let the smallest state in the country shine.

I was set to work with Elijah Stephenson from YouthBuild, an organization whose mission is to "provide young people with opportunities for positive life choices and experiences."

YouthBuild is a national organization, and I was a bit surprised it had taken me until state No. 42 to learn more about one of the most-hands on opportunities around.

Unlike many of the other places I visited, where we often had to brainstorm to come up with one-day volunteer activities, finding something to do with YouthBuild was a cinch.

Visiting on a Saturday, however, meant that most of the staff, including the Executive Director, weren't available, pairing me with the young and agile Elijah and a small group of volunteers.

Our task for the day was pretty straightforward: head to a nearby church to paint a utility room.

The initial plan also included some detail work on some windows, but the Pastor changed his mind, leaving the four of us to simply tackle priming the relatively small, downstairs room.

We walked through the outskirts of Providence, from the YouthBuild facility to King's Cathedral, where we were greeted with Dunkin Donuts, coffee and big smiles.

After the standard pleasantries, we maneuvered downstairs to the room, which was abutted by a small thrift-shop-type area. The room appeared to be primarily a storage area, and we kicked off the day by moving out several shelves and small pieces of furniture, and shrouding a couch in plastic to protect it from the paint.

I tried to strike up conversation with the members of the program who'd joined us, but both were pretty shy, and focused on getting the job done – understandable, considering they surely weren't accustomed to having a globetrotting, shaggy-haired volunteer with a GoPro tag along for the ride.

In what surely wasn't the most exciting live-stream of my summer, I stationed my iPhone on the windowsill and fired up a Meerkat broadcast that was, literally, for the most part, an opportunity to watch paint dry.

Interestingly, though, a few minutes after I began the stream, and, of course, chatted with the handful of viewers who popped by, Elijah received a text from his boss, letting him know that he was home sick – but he was watching us get the job done through the stream.

It was a relatively cut-and-dry day, so far as my trip went – I spent most of the day with a roller in hand, climbing up on a ladder and using my wingspan to detail the corners that some of the younger, shorter volunteers struggled for.

When we were done painting – considerably ahead of schedule – we replaced all the furniture back into the now-white room, said our goodbyes to the Pastor and headed back to the office.

The kids didn't stick around too long – though they'd get full credit for the anticipated hours of the project – and after I wrapped up my interviews with Elijah, I was once again on the road, to finally finish off my exhausting six-states-in-seven-days corridor.

NEXT STOP: Hartford, Conn.

- - - - -

Elijah Stephenson (13:20)

SnapChat Interview (1:37)

"Do you, and when it's hard, hold on. We need you!"

"Just keep smiling. Smiles for Smilow - Lexi"

Aug. 9, 2015 (State #43/50)

HARTFORD, Conn. – Coordinating visits to nonprofits in all 50 states is really, really difficult.

I knew when I scheduled Hartford on a Sunday that this would be one of the toughest days to nail down all summer. In the west, or the southeast, life just seems to move at a different pace, and accommodating a Sunday visit in Boise, or Minnesota, wasn't nearly as tricky as making the ask in the Northeast.

I asked a lot of Robin McHaelen, on one of her busiest days of the year, and she and her team went way above and beyond to shift my Hartford experience from one of my most nerve-wracking to one of my favorites.

Aug. 7 was True Colors' long-scheduled Draguation ceremony, at Theatreworks, a bigtime facility in downtown Hartford. Draguation is the culmination of a summer-long program called Queer Academy, which teaches Hartford's LGBT youth about the long-winded history of gender identity in the United States.

The evening ceremony would feature drag performances by many of the organization's proud youth, with a small reception before and after in the lobby. All things considered, it was quite a production to organize, and here I was, on one of the worst days of the year to request a chunk of the Executive Director's time for a couple of sit-down interviews.

But Robin McHaelen's heart trumped all. She was incredibly gracious and kind off-camera, and when the camera flicked on, she produced the "je ne sais quoi" that only the most polished executives can call upon.

Even with the stress of one of her biggest events of the year just hours away, and chatting with a guy who was starting to feel like he'd been run over by a truck after a full week of nonstop travel, Robin

McHaelen brought it like a true professional, and I am still especially grateful to Robin, as well as Program Director Kamora Herrington and program graduate/volunteer Chris Shropshire for letting me hang out for a while during the morning.

With the clock ticking, I hustled out of the office to the nearest Panera – closed on Sundays – so I hustled to the next-nearest Pandora, to edit my videos together as quickly as humanly possible, so I could swing back around and make it to help out at the Draguation ceremony that evening.

The thought crossed my mind of just heading home to Long Island – where my bed, and more importantly, my family, awaited. I could be home for dinner, but with the way the True Colors team went above and beyond for me that morning, I made the call to stick around Hartford to be able to bounce back and volunteer as long as I could at Draguation.

I aggressively whisked the videos together – a process that, to the T, took about two hours (I'd done it 41 times now) – and squeezed in a phone interview with Newsday, Long Island's signature newspaper, and sped downtown to the facility.

As always, I was there to volunteer however possible, but on this night – with all the other volunteers already pegged into their roles – I came up with a fun, innovative idea that I'm still proud of to this day:

I'd helped set up an oversized NBC banner, almost like a red-carpet concept, where attendees could pose and have their picture taken. The event felt like a big party, and although there was no "traditional" media there, I saw my calling – as the official photographer of Draguation.

Except I wasn't going to print out Polaroids for everyone – instead, I handed out my business card, which featured my SnapChat logo, and snapped a "roll" of photos onto my SnapChat story.

I encouraged attendees – mostly younger, tech-savvy youths – to add me on SnapChat, and screenshot any of the photos from my story that they wanted to keep. It was a fun, creative and engaging way to use the technologies at our collective fingertips to provide tangible value to all the participants.

As the lights flickered and the curtain rose, I had to Irish Goodbye my way to the parking lot and back onto the highway. I was obviously invited to stay – and would've loved to, if it had been any other day of my trip. But with home sweet home just hours away, a job well done in Hartford all around, and the six-states-in-seven-days stretch finally behind me, I was as ready as I'd ever be to hit the road.

NEXT STOP: Huntington Station, N.Y.

- - - - -

Robin McHaelen (14:47)

SnapChat Interview (1:54)

"Never look back, they might be catching up. - Poppa Doc Strub"

"Never stop doing what you're doing. - Cathy Ketcham"

"Try → Know. - Jean"

"Friends are like four-leaf clovers. Lucky to have but hard to find. - Quinn"

"Follow your dreams! - Parker"

"Remember your roots! <3 Your favorite little siski"

"Cut your hair! #longhairdontcare"

"Don't let anyone ever tell you that you can't. - Jim Polansky"

"You can be whatever you want to be. - Frank Petrone"

"Don't worry, be happy. - Mom xoxo"

Aug. 8, 2015 (Bonus Visit!)

HUNTINGTON STATION, N.Y. – At this point, I could've just slept for weeks.

Physically, I was toast. I could hardly remember the last time I had any opportunity to exercise – I'd run some laps in Maine, and lifted some weights at the Courtyard by Marriott in Pittsburgh – and I had just wrapped up an exhausting six-states-in-seven-days whirlwind.

I was in my own, incredibly comfortable bed, at home, with my Mom in the next room, and everything was perfect.

And so, of course, it was time to fire it up for the biggest crowd of the summer.

Here's how it all played out: about a week earlier, I'd sent an email to the office of Town Supervisor Frank Petrone, expressing my interest in meeting him, possibly doing a photo opp, etc.:

"I'm very excited to get back to Long Island next week to visit my family for two days, before setting back out to finish the trip on Aug. 21 in Asheville, N.C.

I'd love to meet you next Monday or Tuesday and tell you a bit more about a Huntingtonian making his way around all 50 states for a good cause. Let me know if you might be available!"

I knew I was coming home for a couple days to rest and relax, but when the Supervisor's communications director, A.J., saw what my trip was about, he understandably pushed to get me to meet up with kids at a program in Huntington.

This was, of course, a great idea – much better than just hanging with Frank for a cup of coffee.

It also required an extraordinary amount of coordination and effort, as well as a ton of energy on my part – things that were, understandably, in short supply, especially on short notice.

I'd planned my visits to all the organizations I'd visited months in advance; I started my outreach as early as February. But when A.J. lept at the chance to put together a special visit for me, at a school that I'd attended as a child, there was, of course, no way I could possibly turn it down.

So, for the first time all summer, I was heading to an event I had absolutely no part in planning. It was kind of nice, in a way, to not have to worry about it – just show up, and you're good! – but also kind of nerve-wracking, to not know what to expect.

So when I showed up, flanked by both my Mom and Dad, and parked behind the Jack Abrams STEM School, I met A.J. and the Supervisor, and I learned I'd be addressing the crowd of kids.

Who totally filled the (giant) cafeteria.

Gulp.

I had no speech planned. I had no gimmicks; no t-shirt cannon; no confetti to throw, no stuffed animals to rely upon.

Nothing.

And, as I mentioned, I couldn't be much more tired if I tried. Six states in seven days had become seven states in eight days, as we double-dipped on New York (I already had Binghamton in the books).

Without having done the planning, and without any real choice in the matter, I took the "stage" – the front of the cafeteria – and awkwardly addressed the crowd.

I've said all along I took the trip with zero regrets, but it sure would've been smart to be more prepared for the "speaking engagement" I had in Huntington. It happened in other states, too: Vermont. Minnesota. And I didn't know at the time, but New Jersey, too.

One of the worst photos of me all summer is when I was talked into learning the whip and nae nae with the crowd – I turned to look to my parents, and shrugged confusedly – because honestly, this was one of the few moments all summer that I didn't feel in control.

All in all, it was an exceptionally fun morning. I did a couple print interviews, and a few TV interviews. The media were even gracious enough to speak to my parents, who I couldn't have been more thrilled to see that day. Notably, my Dad broke down in tears when being interviewed by FOX 5's Jodi Goldberg, a stunning blonde with a million-dollar smile.

I loved meeting so many of the kids in the Project P.L.A.Y. Program, and I got so wrapped up in chatting and playing outside with them that I didn't go through my standard interview process.

I hadn't planned this visit, so I wasn't sure who, really, to talk to – I hate to keep harping on the "it was all a blur" metaphor, but especially being there with my Mom and Dad, all I really hoped to do was re-energize a bit.

It was truly a perfect ending to a summer-long adventure, but there was only one problem:

It wasn't over.

NEXT STOP: Trenton, N.J.

- - - - -

LONG ISLANDER: Huntington Station Native Volunteering

Across Nation in 100 Days

NEWSDAY: Chris Strub Volunteers in 50 States, but Relishes Return to Huntington Station

HUNTINGTON, NY: 50 States in 100 Days Pilgrimage Hits Home

FOX 5 NY: Volunteer Chris Strub is on a Mission to Change the World, One State at a Time

"Live life on purpose!"

Aug. 12, 2015 (State 44/50)

TRENTON, N.J. – Back on the road after a fun couple days at home, I was running purely on guts as the finish line awaited in South Carolina.

And as I headed to visit B.O.Y.D. – which stands for "Building Our Youth's Development," and is also the surname of founder Bruce Boyd – I had absolutely no idea what to expect.

B.O.Y.D., much like Utah G.A.R.D.E.N.S. in Salt Lake City, started as a passion project by a gentleman whose desire to make a change went above and beyond standard volunteerism.

The summertime program was held upstairs in a school building, and my nervousness was only exacerbated when I pulled into the parking lot.

As I circled around the facility, my Honda Accord nearly completely covered in signatures and words of inspiration, I drove past a lawn full of youths marching in lockstep, with some sort of sergeant barking orders.

I knew there was a possibility that group was the B.O.Y.D. youths, and I smirked at myself – actually, pretty much everything I did this summer was at myself, wasn't it – knowing that I was truly prepared for anything, even if I was going to interview a drill sergeant.

Thankfully, the youths I was looking for were to be found inside. Almost as if they had been sent for me – maybe they were? – a group of kids came down the hallway as I asked the front desk attended where to go.

The kids and I made our way back upstairs, through a hallway lined with lockers, to a classroom, where I met Bruce and his wife.

Still not really sure what to expect from the program, I introduced myself to Bruce, made sure to mention that I'd need some time for the interviews, and readied for whatever he had in store for us.

"Come with me," he said, leading us into the classroom next door, and he offered me a seat at the side of the room.

What followed was one of the most interesting 20 or so minutes of the trip: Bruce quieted the classroom, and boy, did they get quiet.

Bruce stood at the head of the class and spoke – and spoke, and spoke. Delivering what seemed more like a well-rehearsed sermon than any type of lesson plan, Bruce weaved in and out of references to various life skills, repeatedly mentioning a t-shirt competition – about which I would learn a bit more later on – and even, at the end, cuing up the unedited introduction to Eminem's "Lose Yourself."

Intrigued, I listened carefully as Bruce's speech continued. With an eye on the clock, but without having offered me any sort of warning, Bruce transitioned into a concise introduction to "a young man who has followed his dreams around the country."

Feeling disastrously unprepared, I did the best I possibly could to capture the tone and the essence of the talk that Bruce had kicked off.

One thing I loved doing with kids around the U.S. was letting them ask questions. It took all the pressure off of me to come up with something rehearsed. But the mood wasn't quite right to open the floor up – the pressure was on me to deliver something moving, that the kids would remember.

It's hard to recall exactly what I said – although I remember calling on a confident-looking girl and asking her what her goals are, to which she didn't have a response – but I kept it together.

When it was over, I made my way back to my chair and took a deep breath. It was tough, but I'd survived – and hopefully given the kids in that classroom something to take away.

With the classroom discussions over, it was time to turn the tables. Bruce knew that I'd be interviewing him, so he invited two students who had expressed an interest in journalism to hang out and each ask me a question.

Adorably, as we set up the cameras, I asked them what they'd be asking, and they both shied away from giving a hint. (One of the questions was, "How are you paying for all of this?"). I thought it was interesting that, even at such a young age, they thought of journalism in a sense where they couldn't allow the interviewee comfort before the cameras were on.

The kids were great, and once I was done answering their questions – and interviewing Bruce for my own channels – I hung out to check out some of the t-shirt designs they'd come up with for the big competition the next night.

I wish I'd had more time to spend with B.O.Y.D., to get an even deeper appreciation for all the great things Bruce and his team do, but the clock was ticking, and after Bruce signed the car, on I went.

NEXT STOP: Wilmington, Del.

- - - - -

Bruce Boyd (12:47)

SnapChat Interview (1:41)

45: WEST END NEIGHBORHOOD HOUSE

"Follow your passion. Everything else will fall into place."

Aug. 13, 2015 (State 45/50)

WILMINGTON, Del. – I think I was beginning to reach the limit of what a lone human being could handle.

Don't get me wrong. I was extremely excited to get to West End Neighborhood House in Wilmington. I knew going in this would be a fun one, and both Development Director Wes Davis and Executive Director Paul Calistro were overwhelmingly friendly, kind and welcoming.

But my mind was reaching a boiling point. And there was, of course, absolutely no turning back now.

Throughout the trip, I felt a little bit bad for the first few states like South Carolina, Georgia and Florida, because my naivete – about the trip, about nonprofits in general, about everything – likely diminished the way I could portray their organizations. It wasn't until I reached Jackson, Miss., and worked with Kiersten Bullock at the YMCA, that I feel like I really hit my stride. (And that was even after working at Youth Rebuilding New Orleans and E.A.T. South in Montgomery, Ala., two of my three favorite orgs of the entire summer.)

But now, I was starting to sympathize in the other direction. I felt like a starting pitcher who was sent out to start the ninth after 125 pitches – I mean sure, I could continue to throw, probably all day, but it probably wasn't the smartest idea in the world.

The last few stops had taken a whole lot out of me, especially the unexpected stop in my hometown. It was absolutely the right thing to do, but I hadn't accounted for it in my planning, and now I was paying the price.

On top of all of that, the reality was starting to set in.

I didn't have a job.

No one was calling me offering me a job.

I had nearly exhausted my credit limit, and there was no way I was sleeping in my car in New Jersey or Delaware, so that was two more hotel rooms to pay for.

My body had absorbed about 13,000 miles in the car, plus the 7,000 or so in the plane to prance between Seattle, Alaska and Hawaii.

I was gassed. I was truly, in every sense of the word, gassed. Sooner or later, it was going to show.

And it started in Wilmington.

Wes had planned a fun activity for me with the kids – learning to dance the robot, as it was, in fact, robotics week. I'd get to do that dancing on camera for the Tri-State news stations – footage that should probably be destroyed forever – so I wanted to get our interviews done before the media showed up.

I sat down in Paul's office with him and Wes, pressed the button on the camera and kicked off the interview.

Or so I thought.

About two minutes into the Q&A – which, remember, I had done almost 50 times over the past three months, without a hiccup – I realized I had set the camera to take photos instead of record video.

Nightmare.

And Paul Calistro – the Executive Director – is a kind and friendly guy, but also the type of guy you don't want to agitate.

I guffawed at my mistake, apologizing profusely, and in the process of reaching toward my camera to fix the problem – spilled a cup of water all over the table in front of us.

What. A. Nightmare.

The Executive Director – the Executive Director!! – reached for some paper towels to wipe up the mess I'd made.

We've all had these moments in our lives where we wanted to just curl up in a ball, crying, and disappear – this was that moment for me.

I was SO tired from six states in seven days. I was SO gassed from an on-the-spot, high-pressure speech the day before in New Jersey. I was SO done with the roads, the Northeast traffic, that I loved avoiding through the first 40 states or so of this whirlwind adventure. I even, for the first time all summer, had to left-parallel-park to get into West End Neighborhood House. It all added up ...

And now, even though I totally should've been an "expert" in all of this by now, I totally effed up an interview with one of the most influential nonprofit executives I'd come across all summer.

Life went on. I survived. Moreso than almost any other person I met this summer, Wes has been super supportive since the trip ended, writing a great LinkedIn recommendation, volunteering for a Blab hangout and even emailing me words of support. After I fumbled my way through a full day at their terrific organization, I'm extra grateful for his kindness and gratitude.

I wish I could say I'd mentally turn things around, but things really wouldn't get much better as I made my way into Maryland.

NEXT STOP: Baltimore

- - - - -

Paul Calistro & Wes Davis (9:21)

SnapChat Interview (1:48)

DELAWARE ONLINE: Traveling Volunteer Visits Delaware on Nationwide Mission

WDEL 101.7FM: Man Volunteering in All 50 States Visits Wilmington

6ABC: Man Volunteering in All 50 States Comes to Delaware

West End NH Press Room Article

Volunteerism in America: Wes Davis

46: LIVING CLASSROOMS

"Don't be afraid to try something new."

"Everyone has been made for some particular work, and the desire for that work has been put in every heart. - Rumi"

"Thank you! Thank you! Thank you!"

Aug. 14, 2015 (State #46/50)

BALTIMORE – I finally broke down.

It was an unexpected double-shot for me in Baltimore. I spent Friday morning at a planned volunteer spot with Living Classrooms, where I weathered the heat and sunshine to help finish building planters for homes in need around the city.

I had a couple of off days scheduled, primarily because I was set to join a half-marathon trail run on Sunday in Germantown, not terribly far from Baltimore.

On Friday afternoon, the call was made to cancel the race due to the "unexpected" heat – perhaps, maybe, a blessing in disguise, given how much of an emotional wreck I'd be by Saturday afternoon.

My volunteer responsibilities in the books, I spent some time with my old friend Jeff Amoros, with whom I was invited to stay that night. He had a prior engagement that evening, which opened me up to complete my responsibilities with my Hard Rock "support" – not sponsorship, because I didn't get paid a dime, but it was nice to catch some free meals around the country.

I was gassed, and the long morning in the heat, and without a water bottle – I'd simply forgotten to grab one last case for the road – left me hurting that night.

The trip was winding down, and save for trying to maximize the final state, I had all my ducks in a row. So when my friend Lee Karchawer asked me to volunteer and help out with Pay Away the Layaway in Dundalk – right outside of Baltimore – I was more than happy to oblige.

The plan came together quickly, and I made it to K-Mart bright and early for the big day.

Pay Away the Layaway, for those unfamiliar – and, please, I encourage you to visit PayAwaytheLayaway.org for more information – is an organization that pays off layaway plans for families in need around the United States.

An "Angel," representing all the donors that make the payoffs possible, surprises families at the store, who have been brought in thinking they have a chance to win a prize of some sort – the kicker, of course, being that all of their layaway plans had been paid off.

My experience with the organization in Dec. 2014, in Easley, S.C., was a huge impetus for taking the second trip in the first place, and so when Lee offered to let me help once again, I was totally in favor.

The only problem this time was that, having traveled through 45 states solo, without a sponsorship, I was flat out of funds.

No problem, of course – the organization would send me the money up front, and I could easily pay off the bills from a bank account.

Sounds simple – until I realized we'd waited too long to wire the money, and it wouldn't clear into my bank account until the following week.

At this point, though, there was no turning back, and so when we started paying off the bills – with the families waiting up front, by the jewelry counter – I ended up mowing through every credit card in my wallet.

It was embarrassing, humiliating and agonizing – 90% through a solo, 50-state volunteerism quest, without the backing of a sponsor, and now wringing every last cent out of every piece of plastic I could find.

All of this was taking place live on Meerkat, too; I had sent a DM to Ryan Dupre, who lives in the Baltimore area, earlier that morning, and he agreed to come out and help with the streaming of the event.

I felt terrible – it was my first time meeting Ryan, and here I was, fumbling through my wallet, sweating and worrying that this smooth, magical moment was in jeopardy.

All the pressure began to weigh on me – the memory of bumbling through a speech in Huntington; the pain of trying to come up with poignant words in New Jersey; the humiliation of camera failure and spilling water with the Executive Director in Wilmington.

And it kept growing: the self-doubt, that I'd never find another good job; the worry, that I wouldn't even make it all the way back to Greenville; the uncertainty as to whether or not this trip was a good idea in the first place.

Everything manifested in the moment, when finally, I could make my way back to the front of the store, to reveal to the patient families, that in fact, we were there to wipe clean all of their debts, and free them of a burden that had weighed so heavily on them and their families.

The joy, the passion, the magic of that moment crashed against the negativity I was feeling in my heart, and I broke.

I just … broke.

I have no idea if Ryan saw me cry; I have no idea if the unknowing store manager saw me cry; I have no idea if the viewers on Meerkat saw me cry.

I found an inch of solitude, in this arena filled with celebration, corporate glee and media, and I bawled my eyes out. Clean-up on Aisle 5, if you will.

At that moment, I couldn't handle the pressure. The pain. The joy.

The agony in my heart, the indecisiveness in my brain, the gravity of everything along this trip that had brought me to this very moment – it all came tumbling out.

You hear it in sports all the time – leave it all on the line, give it everything you've got, etc.

At that moment, I left it all on the line. I had nothing left to give – physically, emotionally, mentally.

I needed a hug.

And there was Ryan Dupre.

Not just to give me that hug, but to offer the most genuine of support. He offered his gratitude for being part of this magical morning – and insisted on taking me to lunch at Richardson Farms, where his girlfriend, Kayla, works.

We arrived and had lunch, and the couple introduced me to the owner of the store. Upon hearing my story, he told me to grab a bag and fill it with absolutely anything I wanted from the store.

I was awash in emotions – again – but I was seeing the light. In that moment, with Ryan Dupre, I truly understood the power of giving – and the power of sharing your story with the world.

This was a young man I'd never met, or even spoken to over the phone, and here he was, in the moment, offering me everything he could, everything I needed to continue my quest.

In that moment, Ryan Dupre represented everything good in the world – and everything good about the live-streaming community. He didn't have to even reply to my DM – much less spend his day helping me, at a moment when I was feeling as weak as ever.

I very graciously thanked them for the offer, grabbed a couple bags of banana chips, and after an emotional signing of the car, I got back behind the wheel.

With a new lease on life, I was ready to tackle the last four states on my list.

NEXT STOP: Charlottesville, Va.

- - - - -

Rebekah Meyer (10:05)

SnapChat Interview (1:33)

BALTIMORE GUIDE: Charitable Quest brings South Carolina man to Living Classrooms

YAHOO PARENTING: Tears Flow When 'Layaway Angels' Surprise Parents

THE BALTIMORE SUN: 'Layaway angels' surprise Kmart back-to-school shoppers in Dundalk

"Stay a kid at heart and you will always have joy."

Aug. 17, 2015 (State 47/50)

CHARLOTTESVILLE, Va. – If there is a nicer entire staff out there than the one Jacki Bryant has compiled at ReadyKids, I'd love to meet them.

With a fresh perspective and renewed sense of energy after a great lunch in Baltimore, and a much-needed day off in Virginia (again, spent sitting at a Panera, working), I was 100 percent ready for a great day – and Jacki and her team delivered.

When I arrived at ReadyKids first thing in the morning, I was greeted by the full staff, of about 15 – including just one guy.

Jacki had arranged for everyone to come out and meet me, over bagels and coffee – of course, I was good with my signature bottle of water – and I was delighted to tell the tale of just how far I'd come all summer.

As much as I loved working with kids all summer long, I often described the trip as "a trip about kids, for adults." I felt much more comfortable speaking with managers, directors and even volunteers about the intricacies of what made their respective organizations stand out in their community, and then offering my perspective from lessons that I'd learned elsewhere.

My "host" for the day, if you will, would be Allison Henderson, whose kind spirit was constantly on display. After introductions, I'd travel with Allison over to one of ReadyKids' remote facilities – in fact, almost all of what ReadyKids does is off of the main premises – before circling back for interviews with Jacki.

It was a perfect plan, albeit slowed a bit when local media showed up for interviews – certainly no big deal by now – but eventually, Allison and I headed to Southwood Mobile Home to help with registration for the ReadySteps program.

It was eye-opening to see the outskirts of Charlottesville, a town typically known for the glitz and glamor of U.Va. In fact, as Allison would explain to me on our way over, Southwood is located just a few blocks past one of the most upscale schools in the city.

The dramatic difference in class structure in such a small geographic area was reminiscent, to me, of Burlington, Vermont – but I had little time to sit and pontificate about such comparisons.

Being that we were a bit later than expected to Southwood – my fault, as I always enjoyed chatting with media, especially print – I only got a few minutes to hang out with some kids, while parents were there to learn more and, hopefully, sign up for the organization's ReadySteps program.

The children almost exclusively spoke Spanish, but the languages of dancing and swinging around colorful streamers are universal. I tried my best to cheer the kids up, using a handful of props available on tables around the small room.

We headed back so I could wrap up my interview with Jacki, the Executive Director, and it went about as well as you could ever expect an interview to go. In my 47th state of the summer, Jacki's relaxed demeanor made me feel as comfortable as I had yet – a delightfully simple and easy day after a challenging two-week stretch.

I got back in the car smiling – heading, of course, to yet another Panera – knowing that I'd found what had to be the friendliest – and more importantly, perhaps the most impactful – youth organization in Charlottesville.

And I still had a few more great states left to go.

NEXT STOP: Charleston, W.V.

- - - - -

Jacki Bryant (11:35)

SnapChat Interview (1:58)

DAILY PROGRESS: 50 Volunteer Stops, 50 States, 100 Days

NBC29: ReadyKids of C-Ville Welcomes Man Volunteering In All 50 States in 100 Days

"Make a BIG difference, give a LITTLE time!"

Aug. 19, 2015 (State #48/50)

CHARLESTON, W.Va. – The hardest part was behind me. I could practically smell the North Carolina-South Carolina state line off in the distance, and I knew my goal was not just attainable, but inevitable now.

I pulled into the parking lot at the Schoenbaum Center not knowing what to expect from Sara McDowell, the Executive Director of Big Brothers Big Sisters of South Central West Virginia.

In fact, I never really knew what to expect when I walked into any of these youth organizations – but rarely was I as impressed as when I met Sara.

Before we even made our way into the BBBS office – of course, I was very familiar with the BBBS model by now, of pairing adult mentors one-on-one with kids with similar interests – Sara was already abuzz about all the exciting things happening around the Schoenbaum Center.

"Huh?" I thought to myself, and as it turned out, Sara was a step ahead of me on that logic.

At the tail end of the trip, especially for a well-connected director like Sara, my visit was a terrific PR opportunity – and, in fact, multiple television stations would come by and chat with both of us about my brief experience in West Virginia.

But, unlike almost every other organization I visited all summer long, Sara insisted on sharing the spotlight with her neighbors in the space.

And so while my visit to West Virginia was "officially" to BBBS of South Central West Virginia, Sara ensured that my brief time there would allow me to experience the entirety of the Schoenbaum Center.

I felt like a dignitary as we moved from office to office, offering intro after intro and hearing a bit about all the different organizations in this collaborative space worked harmoniously to help families in the this blue-collar town.

Unexpectedly, I had the opportunity to hang out with some wonderful kids in a daycare program, where I was able to bring back an idea that I'd begun with months earlier in another Charleston – at the Carolina Youth Development Center in coastal South Carolina. I asked the kids – younger than most that I met during the trip – to sketch me their best representation of West Virginia, as I tried to do the same.

I actually pulled out the puppy eyes for the first time during the trip – when Sara, who had obviously given tours like this before, said it was time to go – and I demurred,

The woman in charge of the entire operation, Loretta Jett Haddad, even took some time to come speak with us, and graciously agreed to participate in both the YouTube and SnapChat interviews.

After a tiring few weeks through the Northeast – even considering the recharge factor of spending time with family – I was genuinely happy to be heading back into the southeast. I've always felt like my mind operates on a southeastern wavelength – thus, my determination to move to South Carolina – and it was clear that Sara and I got along very well, and shared a big-picture, change-the-world mindset necessary to inspire sweeping changes in whatever we do.

Since the trip ended, Sara and I have stayed in contact, and not only because I hope she'll buy us another box of local delicacies – "hot dogs" from Spring Hill Bakery – next time I'm in Charleston.

So much of my trip was about networking – real-life, face-to-face, in-person networking – and there are few who understand and appreciate the value of networking quite like Sara McDowell.

With the car signed, TV interviews wrapped up, a pledge to substantively keep in touch with Sara, and the finish line most definitely in sight now, it was time to revisit my equestrian knowledge with a quick trip up to Kentucky.

NEXT STOP: Lexington, Ky.

- - - - -

Sara McDowell & Loretta Jett Haddad (14:31)

SnapChat Interview (1:39)

"Strive for excellence, be true to yourself."

Aug. 20, 2015 (State #49/50)

LEXINGTON, Ky. – Why I planned it this way, I don't know.

If you review the map of my trip, you'll notice that Lexington is a bit out of the way, for someone heading from Charleston, W.V., to Asheville, N.C. (and, eventually, Greenville, S.C.).

Sometimes, when you draw up a map of your 50-state, 100-day solo adventure, you get a little tired at the end. And instead of slotting Kentucky in my initial jaunt through the southeast – probably right after Tennessee – I earmarked the Bluegrass State as the second-to-last stop on this epic cross-country adventure.

It didn't matter now – I pulled up to Central Kentucky Riding for Hope for what was certain to be an eye-opening day with some great kids – and, some great horses.

Being that it was No. 49, it was going to be incredibly difficult to wipe the smile off my face, no matter what lay ahead for me.

Flash forward about an hour later, through the introductions and a quick tour, and I seriously doubt CKRH has ever seen anyone scoop and transport horse manure with more genuine enthusiasm.

Yes, part of my penultimate volunteer experience of the summer was literally shoveling poop – and I couldn't have been more excited about it.

I cut a relatively quick interview that I'm 90% sure had a horse's actual ass in the background – not sure, I never saw the clip – and spent much of my morning with Sarah, the quintessential country girl who seemingly understood everything there is to know about the equine world.

I was lucky enough to spend my entire time working with the horses, in various capacities, although it was stressed to me that –

much like so many of the other examples throughout the summer – this program, although centered on horses, definitely wasn't all about the horses.

The time the kids got to spend with the horses was essentially seen as a reward, for working hard in the classrooms – which surrounded the stables, and were also filled with kids throughout the day.

So for me – even with the shovel in my hand – a morning with the horses was absolutely a reward.

I loved getting a chance to head outside with Sarah, who insisted on introducing me to the mini horses grazing in a field.

I loved getting a chance to chat with Brian McIntyre, the Administrative Dean of the Stables, a broad-shouldered Southern gentleman with a keen sense of humor and a very welcoming attitude.

I loved meeting Program Director Rachel Baker – even if only for a few moments – because I knew it was her passion that made so much of this great program a reality.

I loved every single minute of my visit to Lexington. It was all terrific, great, and special, and I loved bringing local media attention to a program that helps so many young people, but is also just so genuinely, at its core, a true Kentucky thing.

But – and no one at the Stables, or in Kentucky, should take this the wrong way at all – I was so ready to get back in the car and keep going. I could see the finish line. I was totally riding an adrenaline high all day, that only increased when I got behind the wheel, cranked the Red Hot Chili Peppers and set my GPS to Asheville, N.C.

It was like the moment you slow down from that one final dramatic drop on the best roller coaster in the park, and you can see the finishing gates.

I could sense it. I could feel it. Accomplishment. Celebration. Success. It was inevitable. And it was about to be mine.

NEXT STOP: Asheville, N.C.

- - - - -

Pat Kline & Brian McIntyre (12:48)

SnapChat Interview (1:53)

50: GRAND FINALE - ASHEVILLE

"Unidos Nunca seran vencidos! Get that degree and never let anybody stop you!"

"Don't be afraid to make mistakes!"

"Always believe in yourself"

"Always wonder + ask questions."

"Stay true to yourself no matter what others say."

"PRAY. Trust in the Lord with all your heart!!"

Aug. 21, 2015 (State #50/50)

ASHEVILLE, N.C. – Suddenly, I was ready for more.

This was it! This was finally it! Here I was, in Asheville, N.C. – the lucky city where I would wrap up my 50-state, 100-day adventure.

And instead of gearing down, I was as energetic as I could possibly be.

It was a Friday – my last couple days before turning 30 on Sunday – and I had arranged for at least four organizations to take part in the final day of my adventure.

I had written up a special press release, and sent it not only to the contacts I could find in Asheville, but also all the folks who had done such a great job previewing the trip before it began, in Greenville.

It was a day to celebrate, to live it up, and to make as big an impression on the great little city of Asheville as I could.

I'd made it! I was there! I checked into a "nice" hotel – nothing extravagant, as my wallet continued to cry, but I certainly wasn't going to skimp on the final night – and sorted out my dinner options.

The support was pouring in via Twitter, as the Meerkat community sent every emoji imaginable my way. I felt everything you're supposed to feel when you succeed – elation, confidence, accomplishment, everything. The whole shebang.

As I prepared for dinner, before pressing 'broadcast' to officially close the door on the whole 'first to live-stream in all 50 states' angle, I even got a message from a relatively new friend on Meerkat, Chef Lizette, who'd sent me, through PayPal, enough for me to go get a healthy, enjoyable dinner.

I was modestly familiar with Asheville, having spent a few weeks at a hotel there, covering a management vacancy for the Sbarro at the mall. I wasn't going to get Sbarro, though, and I ended up with a steaming plate of fajitas, and a top-shelf margarita, at Chili's.

I enjoyed my dinner, sipped the margarita – don't worry, just one, and my hotel was just up Tunnel Road – and contemplated what my life would hold ahead.

First, of course, was the following day, the "Grand Finale," where I'd squeeze in as many visits – and mini-interviews – as I could.

But vacuuming my life into a 100-day segment might not be all its cracked up to be, I thought.

I knew I had accomplished something awesome, even if the next day was a total disaster. (It wasn't.)

I also knew there were a ton of questions left to be answered:

What do I do from here?

How am I going to repay the financial debt I've accrued?

Speaking of debt, how can I ever say thanks to the thousands of people that helped me make this trip possible?

Will the girl that I think I might've fallen for in (state redacted) still feel the same way about me?

What's next?

As I write this in mid-December 2015, I still don't know most of those answers. (Except for the girl, that's a big "no.")

I knew there were a lot of things I didn't have – money being the biggest one – but I tried to think beyond that.

I focused on what I did have:

-   Thousands of new friends around the country

-   100 days full of memories that can never be taken from me

-   A car completely covered in words of inspiration from some of the brightest minds in the U.S.

-   The opportunity to tell a story that no one in the world can match

-   The undying love of my family back on Long Island, and extended family around the country

-   The determination to never give up on my dreams, and proof positive that I, literally, could accomplish anything I wanted to, even if it cost me everything I had.

I got as good a night's sleep as I reasonably could, and woke up ready for the Grand Finale.

If all my other visits were "blurs," that Friday in Asheville was a series of blips on a radar screen. I literally raced between six different youth organizations, conducting abridged interviews at each one, starting with Children First-Communities in Schools, and powering through Verner Early Learning; United Way Asheville; Girls on the Run Asheville; Big Brothers Big Sisters of Western North Carolina; before finally screeching to a halt at the Salvation Army Boys & Girls Club of Asheville-Buncombe County.

Unfortunately for them, no local media decided to cover the story. I felt disappointed on that day, only because I always wanted to try and generate the exposure for the various organizations, but the truth was, it was truly the media's loss. It was Aug. 21, 2015 that I felt like I truly accomplished my goal, and I didn't need a television camera to validate anything.

It's hard to describe how I felt, sitting in the parking lot at the Boys & Girls Club, having bid farewell to new Executive Director Haley Shealy and about 30 boisterous, enthusiastic kids.

Much like this book – it was over.

But my personal story was just beginning.

NEXT STOP: Greenville, S.C. (That's it!)

- - - - -

GRAND FINALE - Six Organizations (27:51)
SnapChat Interviews (3:48)

Printed in the United States of America

ISBN 978-1-48359-472-9

- - - - - - - - - - -

To further connect with Chris, feel free to initiate
a conversation on any of the following platforms:

www.Facebook.com/TeamStrub

https://www.linkedin.com/in/chrisstrub

Twitter, Snapchat, Periscope, Musical.ly,
Instagram, Untappd - @ChrisStrub

Want to bring Chris to work with organizations in your community?
Get details at www.TeamStrub.com/IAmHere

To support any of the organizations featured in this book, please
visit their respective websites, which are all listed, by state, for your
convenience on my website: www.TeamStrub.com.

The author accepts full responsibility for any errors in this book,
and would sincerely appreciate any corrections or clarifications.
Please use the email address listed above.

Cover design by Julia Barac - @jingles24.
Made, ironically, in Canada.

229

To see more photos from the #TeamStrub journey, please add Chris
on Instagram: @ChrisStrub.

Thank you.

Made in the USA
Middletown, DE
16 March 2019